THE DIARY OF EDWIN WAUGH
JULY 21ST 1847—FEBRUARY 10TH 1851

The Diary of Edwin Waugh

Life in Victorian Manchester and Rochdale

1847 – 1851

edited and abridged by
Brian Hollingworth

The Diary of Edwin Waugh:
Life in Victorian Manchester and Rochdale 1847–1851

Copyright © Brian Hollingworth, 2008

ISBN 10: 1-904244-49-1

ISBN 13: 978-1-904244-49-3

Designed and Typeset by Carnegie Book Production, Lancaster
Printed and bound by Cpod, Trowbridge, Wiltshire

Contents

Introduction

The name of Edwin Waugh may be little known today, but to an earlier generation, at least in parts of Lancashire, his name was as familiar as that of Charles Dickens or Thomas Hardy. In the later part of the nineteenth century his poetry and prose writing in the Lancashire dialect received widespread recognition – he was often spoken of as 'the Lancashire Burns' – and he became, within his own lifetime, the acknowledged leader of a flourishing school of local literature. Anyone concerned with the development of vernacular writing in the nineteenth century will be drawn to the work of Waugh, and must be impressed by its quality and extensiveness.

It is fortunate, therefore, that the Central Reference Library in Manchester, has in its archives considerable material concerning this important local figure, and particularly interesting that, amongst this material, is the extensive diary which Waugh kept between 1847 and 1851. Here I am presenting an edited and abridged version of this diary. I believe it has a strong intrinsic interest as a personal testimony of a particularly intimate kind, as an insight into the struggles of a 'working-class' aspiring writer, and as a document of social history during an extremely active decade in the development of the Industrial North.

Edwin Waugh was born in Rochdale in 1817, and died at New Brighton in 1890. He was the son of a shoemaker, Edward Waugh, whose ancestors came from the Scottish borders, and Elizabeth Haworth, who had previously been married to a well-to-do handloom weaver, and had strong connections with the early Methodist movement. His father died when Edwin was nine. In their poverty, the family were reduced to living in a cellar – not an uncommon fate in those difficult times. His mother earned money selling shoes on the Rochdale open market.

These unhappy events have encouraged some earlier readers to envisage Waugh as a romantic stereotype of the successful self-educated man, rising by his own industry and persistence from the mass of down-trodden working people to carve an unlikely career for himself in the alien world of Victorian literature. Such an image would certainly appeal to Waugh himself, whose own sense of vocation towards a literary career, and sense of crippling failure too, is well illustrated in this Diary. It may also appeal to some readers today who will see here the struggles of the self-taught man to distance himself from his class origins and seek for respectability through his work and literary aspirations.

Nevertheless, such a picture would be over-simplified, and depend upon assumptions concerning class and convention which are too broadly conceived. Waugh's background was scarcely 'typical working class' if such a concept can actually be identified in early nineteenth-century urban society. He could look to his mother's first husband as a man of substance, and to his father as a man who had been educated at Rochdale Grammar School. He had inherited from his mother the strong urge to respectability and personal improvement which distinguished the Methodist movement.[1] Reading and writing were not unexpected discoveries to him, nor did Waugh struggle to literacy against all the odds. Waugh did, in fact, attend school sporadically both before his father's death and afterwards, and his early job in Holden's Rochdale bookshop enabled him, if only in unofficial ways, to continue his literary education. In its own humble fashion, the early life of Waugh resembles that of his more famous contemporary, Charles Dickens, and Waugh's experiences as a cellar-dweller can be seen as a parallel to Dickens's experiences in the blacking factory. In both cases, these experiences represented obstacles to the smooth educational progress which might have been desired; but they were fortuitous and in no way represented, for either writer, the starting point of their literary aspirations, or a guideline to their self-perceived social position.

On the other hand, there was nothing in Waugh's social background to suggest that he would become a creative writer, and it would be absurd to argue that these early years were a positive preparation for

[1]   Milner G. *Edwin Waugh*. Manchester Literary Club Papers 1893

such a career. Waugh's entry into the literary world came comparatively late in life, came uncertainly and fitfully, despite all his ambition, and reflected the lack of confidence and influential social contact which was the legacy of his humble background.

His first real breakthrough as a writer did not come until five years after the time covered in this diary, when he was thirty nine years of age. Only then, in 1856, did the Manchester Examiner publish his dialect poem *Come Whoam to thi' Childer an' Me* to give Waugh, at long last, a taste of success, and instant popularity both locally and further afield. Waugh was given a guinea for the copyright, and it was the first piece of verse he had ever been paid for.[2]

Partly we can attribute this success, when it came, to the insatiable Victorian appetite for the sentimental. The poem records a woman begging with her husband to return to his family, instead of wasting time and money at a fair. It celebrates those hearth and home virtues which became so dear to the Victorian sense of propriety, which Waugh himself idealised, and which, as this diary movingly records, he distressfully failed to find in his own married life. Yet, the poem's significance in Waugh's literary career was not only that he had struck a sympathetic chord with the Victorian reading public, but that, at long last, he had found his authentic voice. In the dialect of southern Lancashire he could confidently and genuinely speak and write. Before this time his aspirations were firmly towards poetry and prose in the standard dialect, and success had just as firmly eluded him. Now, and especially in the years up to 1870, Waugh produced a great number of Lancashire dialect poems and prose pieces which have considerable literary merit, and he stood in the vanguard of a great resurgence of Lancashire writing which made it one of the preeminent regional literatures of the Victorian age.

Within such a context this diary proves especially interesting since it so accurately and privately records, before he achieved any success, Waugh's search for a style, and a way to communicate which could be his own. It is remarkable how the tone, the pace, the intensity, even the handwriting of the diary can vary from page to page. On several occasions Waugh seems to be engaged in a writing exercise. He embarks upon set-piece descriptions in a sub-Dickensian style, which have some

[2] Waugh E. Unpublished Pieces MS F828.89W15 Manchester Central Library

charm, and give us interesting glimpses of Manchester life, yet remain uninspired and cold. His description of the flower morning (Saturday May 13th 1848), for instance, is a fascinating account of bygone customs, yet it seems strangely affected and deliberate, especially for a diary entry. Later in the diary, however, there are fine set-piece descriptions of his day-excursion by train to Blackpool (September 27th 1849) and his visit to Knott Mill Fair which are much more compelling, though still definably self-conscious and straining for effect.

Clearly Waugh used his diary, not merely to record the incidents of everyday life, but also to practise the writer's craft. Frequently, though he is apparently writing for himself alone, he will amend his first version of an incident to give his style more polish, or to tone down too intense an expression of feeling. Much of this diary seems to be written for a public as well as a private audience.

Yet the diary also shows ample evidence of those talents which were finally to establish Waugh as a successful writer. He is at his most engaging when he does not strive for effect, but rather when the events he is describing so take hold of his imagination that he drops all literary pretensions and writes simply and directly. So the account of his quarrels and his reconciliations with his wife remain a moving testimony. He commands our attention also when he allows his natural curiosity about the habits and speech of 'Lancashire folk' to have free rein. This curiosity, and the examples he gives of Lancashire speech, markedly increase as the diary proceeds. It is his vivid chronicles of conversations in pubs and offices, in shops and meeting halls, which are most memorable and become the staple of his later published work.

Those who know something of Waugh's subsequent career will here recognise a kind of psychological division which remained with him to his dying day. On the one hand we have the aspiring man of letters, the admirer of Burns, Scott, Emerson and Wordsworth, hoping to produce worthy and well-wrought works of literature. On the other is the 'real' Waugh – the sensitive recorder of the day-to-day life of working people: the artist attuned to the cadences and expressions of vernacular speech. Such a division indicates Waugh's continuing uncertainties and struggles as a writer, even after he became relatively successful.

If Waugh's apprenticeship as a writer had been less difficult, if he had received a good schooling, and made the right social contacts, no doubt these uncertainties would have been resolved. The irony is – a common irony for the 'self-taught' writer – that this resolution would have buried those talents which Waugh ultimately put to such good use. An orthodox literary background could only have inhibited his affinity with the ordinary, the colloquial, the vernacular. Waugh had enough learning to distrust his attraction to the dialect and its speakers, but, fortunately, he had not so much that he lost touch with them.

The diary itself, as will become evident, was written at a difficult time in Waugh's life. After his early apprenticeship in Holden's bookshop, Waugh had left Lancashire to travel the country as a journeyman printer.[3] In 1844 he returned to Rochdale, working once more for Holden, and then for a printer called Norris. After a brief courtship, and against the wishes of her family, he married Mary Ann Hill in May 1847, and shortly afterwards, as the diary records, he found himself out of work.

The marriage was not a happy one. There is evidence enough in these pages of Waugh's strong affection for Mary Ann, and the number of reconciliations and fresh starts recorded here would speak for a strong affection on her side also. But there were too many differences of temperament for them to be permanently compatible.

It is hard to comment upon where faults lay. Waugh speaks disparagingly of Mary Ann's slatternliness, her fecklessness, and the baleful influence of her family on their relationship. On the other hand, there is no evidence that Waugh provided that steadiness of character, industry and companionship which, by the ideals of his own writing, should have been the male part of the marriage contract. Moreover, reading between the lines in Waugh's detailed account of their meeting at the Turf House, his own attitude seems to have been quite as stubborn and uncompromising as the behaviour he attributes to Mary Ann. To be married to a writer is bad enough; to be married to a writer who is in his thirties, penniless, unsuccessful, and with no prospect of success, must have been a daunting prospect for an ordinary Lancashire girl, however well organised she might have been in domestic matters. If there is one dominant theme in the diary it is that of persistent debt – and constantly broken resolutions to break free from debt. This is hardly the basis for a happy relationship.

[3] Robertson W. *Old and New Rochdale and its People*, Rochdale 1881

Waugh's detailed account of the break-up of his marriage will go far to destroy any lingering romantic dreams, conjured up by Waugh and his contemporaries, about the comfort of Victorian firesides, and the insignificance of Victorian sexual passion. But in Waugh's case, especially, his story is valuable since it offers a personal and dramatic view of a living relationship between two people from a sector of society, and from a region of England, often ignored by social commentators.

The story drags on beyond the limits of this diary, but it has no happy ending. Waugh records in the diary the birth of their first child, and two more were born later, but eventually the rift between himself and Mary Ann became permanent, and, from 1856 onwards there seems to have been no real contact between them. Yet Mary Ann Waugh, designated as Head of Household, married and with no occupation, was still living in Lower Shore at the time of the 1881 census.

Another point of real interest in the diary is Waugh's account of his work for the Lancashire Public Schools Association during these years. As he records, after losing his job with Norris, and working very briefly on the *Courier* in Manchester, he was finally engaged as Assistant Secretary of the newly-formed organisation in mid-September 1847. It was an appointment of great significance in Waugh's career. Work with the Association brought him to Manchester, where most of his future life was spent, and it was work with the Association which at last brought him to the fringes of the local literary establishment. His immediate superior during much of his time there was Francis Espinasse, a Scotsman who claimed friendship with Carlyle, and himself nursed literary ambitions. On the Committee of the Association were the Reverend William McKerrow, Alexander Ireland, and Thomas Ballantyne who were all proprietors of the *Manchester Examiner and Times* where, sporadically, Waugh's writing began to appear from this time onwards.

The Lancashire Public Schools Association itself was a significant, but ultimately unsuccessful, attempt to encourage a local (and later a national) system of publicly-provided education. From the 1830s onwards Government grants had been available to further elementary education, but these had always been channeled through the various religious bodies which were establishing schools, and reflected a middle-class consensus that instruction in religion was the paramount concern in bringing learning to the masses.

One weakness of such a system of provision was that religious bodies did not, and could not, cater for all the children in the rapidly expanding industrial areas. Nevertheless Sir James Graham's bill of 1843, which attempted to make some educational provision compulsory in workhouses and textile mills, had foundered on the opposition of manufacturers and those religious objectors who believed that the established church was too much favoured by its provisions.

With this background the Lancashire Public Schools Association (L.P.S.A.) was established in July 1847 to 'promote the establishment of a general system of secular education in the County of Lancaster'.[4] The key features of their scheme were that local areas should be given power to tax themselves to provide schools and control expenditure, and that 'all catechisms and creeds were to be strictly excluded, but religious teaching was to be based on selections from the Scriptures'[5]

It was not until 1870, with Forster's Act, that a national system on a somewhat similar fashion was finally inaugurated. Even then the Act involved considerable compromises with the various religious lobbies, and it is evident that the L.P.S.A. was well before its time in its attempts to provide a 'secular' education in the late forties and early fifties. The diary is much concerned with the religious controversy which 'the Plan' aroused, and, in the long run, Parliament lacked the will and popular middle-class support to pass the necessary legislation which the L.P.S.A. sought.

Nevertheless, despite all the obstacles, the Association did inspire great devotion and enthusiasm in Manchester and beyond, and, after such hiccups as Waugh records when it seemed they could not afford to pay his wages, it went from strength to strength during the period when Waugh was associated with it. On the 30th October 1850, Waugh describes the meeting where it was enlarged to the 'National Public Schools Association'. It remained an active and important influence for educational reform at least until 1855, and was not actually disbanded until 1862.[6]

Waugh's accounts of meetings, and details of the Association's politics may not be of immediate interest to the modern reader, but his

---

[4] Maltby S. E. *Manchester and the Movement for National Elementary Education*, Manchester 1918 p. 68.
[5] ibid. p. 69
[6] ibid. p. 81

work in collecting subscriptions, and generally furthering the cause, brought him into contact with a wide circle of people, of various ranks in society, and involved an amount of travelling on the pristine railways of South Lancashire (the Manchester to Leeds railway east of Rochdale had only just been opened) which adds yet another dimension to the interest of his diary.

1848, the first full year which Waugh records, was 'the year of revolutions' – a time of extensive political unrest throughout Europe. It was the year of *The Communist Manifesto*, the Paris Commune, and intensified Chartist activity in Britain. Manchester, and its surrounding area, the centre of the Industrial Revolution, was inevitably caught up in the volatility of the year, both in politics and literature. It was in Manchester in 1845 that Engels produced *The Condition of the Working Class in England* and in 1848 Gaskell wrote *Mary Barton*. The sufferings of the Manchester operatives during 'the hungry forties' have become legendary.

There is some reflection of these stirring times in the diary, though there is no great radical fire bursting forth. Waugh's sympathies are clearly with the oppressed working man, the poor and the destitute. His description of the frail woman begging in the shoe shop in the middle of Manchester (19th September 1848) is one of the most moving episodes in the diary, and that is only one of several sympathetic references to the plight of the penniless in these difficult times. He describes also, critically but not antagonistically, his visit to the home of Bowker, the Chartist, in Miles Platting. He attended, and strongly approved, the lectures given by the radical Henry Vincent during the spring of 1848. Nevertheless, we do not gain from the diary, any feeling of imminent political and social crisis – no feeling that we are on the verge of that major social breakdown which many people may have anticipated. It is notable also that, though he mentions cholera in general, he never mentions the specific outbreak which occurred in Manchester in 1849. And again, though, as a Rochdale man, he was friendly with the founders of the fledgeling Cooperative movement – Jem Daly, the first Secretary of the Pioneers was indeed a close friend, and the diary records significant meetings with William Mallalieu – his expressed involvement with them never moves beyond passive sympathy for their ideals.

Rather than offering visions of social crisis, therefore, this diary reminds us that, even in critical times, life for the majority may seem no more than the inevitable continuation of the familiar – the daily struggle to make ends meet, to keep going in a careless, or often hostile environment. This seems the lasting impression of Waugh's account. Here we see an ambitious, yet rapidly ageing 'young man', newly-married, but already plunged deep in matrimonial distress, deep in debt, and never secure in his job. Here is a struggle to keep alive. For all its occasional attempts at fine writing, it appeals most as the intensely personal story of an ordinary man. For all the great public events happening around, it is an intimate account of personal sorrows and joys – and perhaps it is all the more engaging for that very reason.

Acknowledgements

I would like to thank Michael Powell, Librarian of Chetham's Library, Manchester, for his help and support in producing this edition of Waugh's diary. He provided much valuable background material, and, in particular, a copy of a transcription of the diary which Martha Vicinus made some thirty years ago. Given the vagaries of Waugh's handwriting, this was very useful in cross-checking his exact usage at several points.

Thank you also to Professor Vicinus herself for her encouragement concerning this venture, and her permission to consult her transcription. And to Professor Florence Boos of Iowa University for her valuable comments on the text and commentary.

Thank you to George Kelsall for his support, and for showing me many of Waugh's haunts around Hollingworth Lake, Littleborough, Shore and Rochdale.

Patrick Joyce in his book *Democratic Subjects* (Cambridge 1994) provides a detailed and interesting commentary on Waugh and the significance of this diary.

Again, some twenty five years ago, the Librarian of the Central Library in Manchester provided me with a photocopy of the entire diary which has formed the basis for this edition. Thank you.

Brian Hollingworth

The numbers in the text refer to the page numbers in the original diary.

The diary opens with cuttings from newspapers concerning Emerson's lectures on 'Reading' and on 'Goethe – The Man of Letters' given at the Manchester Athenaum. These lectures, as the diary later reveals, greatly influenced Waugh. There is also a cutting on 'The Use of a Diary' and a brief poem before a longer poem 'To my New Book'. Then there are further quotations from Bacon and Emerson, and some very faint entries which appear to date from after his appointment as Assistant Secretary of the Lancashire Public Schools Association.

The diary proper opens on Page 9. Then Waugh was living at Peanock by Hollingworth Lake near Littleborough and working for the Rochdale printer Norris. He was in a very depressed state of mind and much of the writing, from his first entry on Wednesday, July 21st 1847 concerns his misery and lack of direction. Nevertheless, some interesting accounts concerning local events soon begin to emerge.

[13] **SUNDAY JULY 25TH** [1] – ... Chat with old Buckley and his wife. Great preparations for 'th'Rushbearing'. – Jamie's account of the progress of the new Reservoirs at Greenbooth. – anecdotes illustrative of the life and characteristics of that remarkable branch of the human family called the 'Navvy' or navigator – from their formerly being much employed, and often in great numbers in works of Inland Navigation. – Jamie's specimen of their mode of time-keeping – The square being their mark for a day's work, two sides of a square is half a day's work, and one fourth of a square – a quarter of a day's work; – and the dot . the mark for one hour's work – it reminds me of a humorous incident that happened in the court house once, when an old woman that kept a public house sued some fuddler for the 'shot' he owed her. – She was requested to produce her book of accounts, and a messenger was despatched for it – He entered the court again ' wi the buttery dur

---

[1]   Waugh's writing of dates in the diary is very irregular but I have not standardised them.

up oo his shielder, cover't o'er wi' Great O's an little o's an straight strokes /'s an crosses+ ole so' – This was [14] her day book, and these hieroglyphics made up her system of book keeping, and a common one among her class ...

Waugh, living in this rural retreat, as a man who wanted to make his name as a writer, also displays a close interest in nature and goes into considerable detail concerning the flora round the lake, using appropriately romantic language. His account of the local General Election in the summer of 1847 follows, though it is notable that, until he began to work in Manchester his grasp of calendar time is decidedly wayward.

[18] **WEDNESDAY, JULY 29.** [*actually the 28th*] – A Tory Candidate brought before the Electors of Rochdale under the patronage of the lord of the Manor. – Busy in the office with the long rambling address. – drunken copy. – endless and annoying corrections and revisions. _ Interior of the lord of the Manor's Mansion. – The Dining Room. – The Littleborough parson, The Coroner, and the Barrister Candidate at Supper, with the bluff sportsman that now holds a title and inheritance that formerly, from time immemorial ['*Very ancient*' *deleted*] was held by the proud Byrons, barons of Rochdale, and which was bought from Lord Byron, the poet of Missolonghi. – A crowd of electioneering guzzlers and creeping slaves that hang about the skirts of the Tory Party here, – that dog the heels of those slaves that love to have slaves about them – [19] despicable reptiles devoid of sense and principles, that creep about and clamor [*sic*] for dirty work and do it shamelessly, dishonorable [*sic*] brutish dogs, that lap up every fool's slops, – that love knavery, and filch recklessly as the [*filthy*' *inserted*] reward of their filthy business.

THURSDAY, JULY 30. [*the 29th*] – The office still storming with the chatter of whiskered monkies [*sic*], the fume of cigars, the clashing of pots, and the splashing of ale, and the oaths and ribaldry of beastly 'Swillickers'. – I overheard one of these pigs in the garb of gentlemen say, – alluding to a late debauch, that 'his inside wur uz raw uz a collop'.

FRIDAY JULY 31 – [*the 30th*] The Tory candidate, finding there was not the remotest chance of his election, vanished like a vapour, leaving behind him as a legacy, and a remembrancer to the Electors, a farewell address, as incomprehensibly vague and untranslatable into common sense as that first long tipsy rhodomontade of his, which born among the fumes of wine, still seems to stagger about on the paper in its drunken incognito – a life-long monument of bacchanalian literature – hurrah – [20] But he is fled; and left a better man to bear the representative honours of the town, – and to bear its labours too, for this man was more sought for than seeking such elevation – and accepted the trust only that he may labor [*sic*] honourably [*sic*] in it, and not for the empty name.[2]

A few lines of poetry 'Fare thee well and if for ever' celebrate this departure.

[21] **SATURDAY AUG 1** [*the 31st July!*] – Sunny, smiling August! Sportsmen begin to rub up their girths[?] and prepare their guns and dogs, and themselves, by preparatory exercise, for the moor sport on the 12th – The village 'Rushbearings' come on in quick succession now. – Milnrow 'Rushbearing' begins tomorrow (Sunday forsooth) – but it is a fading relique of a very ancient festival of the Church! – I am tired today with the confusion of the week.

SUNDAY AUG 2 [*the 1st*] – So fagged that I slept longer than usual this beautiful Sunday morning – Sunday morning! – The very name warms my heart with a pure reverential joy! – The very name is calm and lovely in my ears! – O grief that such an heaven-sent Sacrament should be misused and desecrated by me! – I have missed the beautiful service of the church this morning again! – I took a book – after I had washed and breakfasted – and went into the fields to read! – The boat came dancing over the lake. I hailed it and went in. – It was nearly filled with Sunday School girls, who sang some [22] fine hymns so beautifully, that as I sat with my legs across the prow of the boat, in my white shirt sleeves, and feeling so perfectly clean and glad from head to foot in body, – and watching the grand sunlight gleam in innumerable rays athwart the clear deeps wc sailed over – and listened to the echoes of sacred song among the woods above, from so many sweet voices, I felt as if I was accompanying a cargo of angels to that amaranthine land

---

[2]   In the event, W. Sharman Crawford, the Liberal candidate, was elected unopposed as MP for Rochdale in 1847. (see entry for 11th May 1848 below)

'Where a leaf never dies from the still blooming bowers,
And the bee banquets on through a whole year of flowers.'

The book I had with me among the woods and fields today, was a most inspiring one, – 'The pursuit of knowledge under difficulties.' – I was in the boat from eleven till half-past three. I found John Stephens sitting on the bank of the lake under an ash tree making a Sketch – He had my Moore's Melodies in his pocket, – and had just returned from his Irish tour. His description of his journey and sojourn in ' Green Inisfail was bare and unanimated [23] as his language commonly is, compared with the interest of the subjects of his conversation, and even in comparison with the interest they have for him. – But the want is not so much in his heart's feeling and perceptions as in his power of language. – He is more akin to the silent spirits that fret themselves under constitutional conversational hindrances. – Yet he has more thought and feelings than many very eloquent babblers. – We strolled about the lake in a very delightful, easy, unconventional ramble among the wild flowers that we both love exceedingly.

[*More rhapsodising on nature follows ...*] We took tea at the Old Farm and walking together across 'Blackrod Hill', as the summer Sun was sinking toward Brown Wardle Hills; –

'each took off his several way
Resolved to meet some ither day.'

It is evident that at this time Waugh had serious money problems, and his relationship with his employer Norris was on the point of breaking down. He seems to have been going to work only intermittently during the following week, feeling ill, reading and studying Latin. He claims that Norris's business is about to collapse through his employer's 'reprobate habits' and 'increasing inattention to business' [24]. Things came to a head on the following Friday. It may seem significant that the first mention of Waugh's wife, Mary Ann, is an assessment of her value as a wage-earner.

[25] **FRIDAY, AUG 6** – ... Norris sent up such insulting messages to me today by the lads that at last I flew into an ungovernable passion upon his making his appearance himself to satisfy his suppositions. In the midst of the thundering eruption he told me in his ludicrously pompous manner, to lay down my composing-stick and leave his employ – and so exasperated was I with his whole manner and tone,

and sense of foregone insult silently [*word missing*] – that I dashed the stick and composition together upon the floor, and should have struck him down had not his voice changed to a beseeching and terrified one – I felt an irresistible indignation at the mean advantages which the foolish whelp had taken of my difficult position with regard to money matters – He went downstairs, saying my wages would be left in the shop – I went down instantly, and the lad told me that I was call [*sic*] in the morning for them. – I called in the middle of the following forenoon. – Norris was in with several gentlemen. – He said 'Edmund has your money, Edwin, but he's gone out; – you can come in again!' – I went out musing on the inauspicious and disordered state of my affairs but still more hopeful and glad than ever before in such circumstances, or in the contemplation of them. – I feel greater confidence in my ability to deal with this wild wide world of ours. In the first place, then, my wife, however unfortunate she may have been in wanting almost entirely the grace and the power – the inestimable blessing of a refined education, – nay in wanting almost totally the commonest school education! – she has had the blessing of this teaching – she has this dignity, and no inconsiderable one that she can get her own living by the work of her hands, and without much discomfort …

There follows what Waugh himself calls 'a digression from the road I was travelling on' [28] concerning the evils of 'polite' education for girls before he returns to his main theme …

I went to the shop again for my money – Norris said 'Edmund had not come in yet,' – but, on going upstairs for payday hat and books and other things I found him there, and sent him into the shop for my money, which I found he had not got – I pocketed the cash [29] and walked off, – I spent the afternoon at my sister's translating Latin Sentences in Valpy's Delectus[3] – I went into a little flourishing magazine shop kept by a man who used to work in the hand-loom, and could hardly even now write his own name, and who commenced his business with three or four shillings in some obscure nook of the town, but who, by prudence and steadiness had overcome every seeming

---

[3] Richard Valpy's *Delectus Sententiarum et Historiarum* was a popular Latin textbook of the time. Mentioned in Anne Bronte's *Agnes Grey* (1847) Chapter 7.

obstacle to improving that worldly condition which to such masses of working men of like condition seems a hopeless unconquerable condition of life-long slavery. He had steadily and slowly progressed, and had won for himself more pleasure and leisure, more physical happiness, – more intellectual improvement, – even though this was not the good he sought for – and more freedom and grace of position in relation to the restless, selfish work of competing toilers and traders that he dwells among ...

The panegyric continues ...

[30] I felt the advantage this man, even so dead in intellect and soul, has over me with his practical prudential wisdom and steadiness –

SATURDAY AUG 8 [*the 7th*] – No Latin today – [*a reference to his wife is here crossed out*] – Desultory reading in the magazines and newspapers – My wife and I walked home very late, laden with provisions and clean clothes – Arrived at Peanock, wet and weary, at midnight.

SUNDAY, AUG 9 [*the 8th*] – The day was very wet, and I was very ill – I lay in bed writing till my head whirled round in a sickly mass – I got up about four o'clock in the afternoon, wrote three scraps of rhyme, – and remained up till about nine o'clock when I went back to bed with right good will. – at my wife's request I read a beautiful prayer written by Old Wesley for Sunday evening. – Noble Wesley! – O God my sins and infirmities! ...

[31] **MONDAY, AUG 10.** [*the 9th*] – Still ill –

An attempt at a poem follows then:

Stayed at home till noon, then went to the town to my Latin lesson. – Walked to the Bridge, with the intent when I started off of calling upon H – and seeking employment in his counting house – but so many conflicting considerations spring up in my mind and my heart so revolted against the counting, the man, and the occupation, that I was [32] not displeased to find him out, and I came away, determining to reconsider the matter and wait a day or two.

TUESDAY AUG 10 – At home till noon – Went to town at noon – Latin lesson – And a lesson from my mother too, with a great deal of sense and feeling in it. – My mind distracted with the gloomy aspect of my affairs – Bills rushing out their corners with very saucy, imperative notes attending them. –

WEDNESDAY, AUG 11 – Made a list of all the monies I owe, and found that I am in debt to the amount of thirty pounds, and I shall have to sell all my books nearly to pay it, – if I do not find employment soon. – I went to Bury in the afternoon.

THURSDAY, AUG 12 – Wrote till the middle of the afternoon – Wrote a list of the names of all my books – to town for Mary Ann at night. – My heart grows worse disgusted every day with my follies, and the downhill [?] – The lights of hope and faith seem put out for ever in me, and I am enveloped in gloom – My soul declines. – I am growing cold-hearted and miserably forlorn. –

[33] **FRIDAY, AUG 13** – [*The entry is taken up with extensive and continued reflections on his depressed state of mind.*]

[34] **SATURDAY, AUG. 14** – I was visited by John Stephens before I had got out of bed this morning. I shouted to him through my bedroom window – telling him that I would follow him down to the waterside in a few minutes. – I dressed and went out – I [*sic*] was a beautifully fresh, clear-aired and sunny morning! – I found him under a thorn-shade sketching. – He had heard of my leaving Norris, as he happened to call last Saturday morning when Norris told him I was not there, – I had left him last night – that I owed him money, and many other people, all over the town, I owed money to, and he added many other slanderous and mean-spirited remarks which I did not expect from him meanly as I think of him. Stephens pressed me to go to breakfast with him. – After breakfast, I was left with Mrs. Blackett, an aged and excellent lady, of most attractive [35] conversation and manners – she would appear much deformed in person, but the intelligence and courtesy of her conversation and manner – the riches of her internal and external experience – the polish of her education, not paraded offensively for show but shining through and enhancing with its grace and force her fine natural common sense in the simplest act and word, – as the sunlight enhances its glory by shining through the stained glass of some grand old cathedral window – her devout character, her fine cultivated mind, her kindliness, – and the humanity of her sympathies lead one insensibly to love her, and to forget completely that she is not beautiful

in body as in soul! – dull and cheerless as I felt, I listened to her advice and her conversation with a more attentive and grateful ear than she conceived of. – God bless her! ...

There follow more extensive self lacerations and appeals to God for help in overcoming his shortcomings. Such reflections cover Waugh's entries over the next three days.

[39] **TUESDAY AUG 17TH** – Wrote a few verses of rhyme today. – If I had opportunity and leisure, I am ambitious above all earthly things to become an eminent poet – to be a fine writer, – but above all, to become in heart and head worthy of the name of a poet. – but my present efforts are rude enough to dishearten my soul not born with a predisposition to the habit of rhyming. –

WEDNESDAY AUG 18. – Read Carleton's Tale of the late Irish famine – 'The Black Prophet' – a terrible revelation! The statistical facts of this sweeping calamity, as stated in the newspapers, were dreadful – but the details are horrifying beyond imagination – they infinitely excel conception. – The bare fact of 2 million and a half of human hearts gradually gnawing and chilling away to the coldness of death makes one shudder with horror at the pitiable and revolting agonies and wretchedness which the heavens must have looked upon. – It is impossible to depict it adequately in words! A nation swept into the grave! –

THURSDAY, AUG 19TH [*More melancholy reflections...*] [40] Went to Mr. Bright's house to enquire for employment in his counting house. – An infernal diffidence shackles me in the transactions of such business as that. He told me there was no hope of employment in their place, the Cotton business requiring so few bookkeepers compared to the woollen and other businesses – He had however some knowledge of Gadsby of Manchester and London the League Printer and would use his interest with him in my behalf – and he would write to me on his return from Manchester on Tuesday next, when he expected to see Gadsby – and he would then inform me with what success he had asked for me. Latin lesson today. 'The circumstance is nothing, the success is all'

I overheard two weavers conversing and one said to the other, ' Aw tel tho wot Jem o Robin's a greadly wastril o gates – Aw wunder at thers nowt tags him wa he coms whom so lot ov a mornin' 'Tag him, be damn'd, [41] he stops so lat whol bwoth gud 'uns un th'ill uns us o sided. Thir tir't o watchin o'th'durty devoul. – een i'thir'n to catch him, thid'n let him gu agen – he's a dam'd deevel worse thur this wants any ' – Few o'th' oud Surs. –

THURSDAY AUGUST 17 – [*this date doesn't fit in easily*] Went to my Latin lesson today. I am delighted even with what is called the drudgery of learning this classical language and if I live shall be eager to master it. Smith, hearing of my probable removal from the town told me that if I had attended rather more regularly I should by this time have been able to translate fluently and well – But I have had 'too many irons in the fire' this last year – and some of the most useful – this among that number which have allowed to burn to cinders – Wisdom is a plant of exceedingly slow and difficult growth in some soils ...

Waugh then makes an elaborate comparison between the state of agriculture in Ireland and his own lack of intellectual progress, and introspection fills the next two pages.

[44] **FRIDAY AUG 18** – [*August 20th*] Began to read 'The Pilgrim's Progress' again. This book was an especial friend of my extreme youth. It then fascinated me as a most marvellous tale! The perpetual succession of wonderful characters and incidents – the beautiful truth and simple life-like naturalness of the language charmed me exceedingly –

I saw Holden, and in my confused ungainly manner in such affairs, I asked him for employment. He inquired why I had left Norris. I told him. He said we never agreed well and he expected we should not remain long together. He could not employ me in his Counting House just now but he thought if he could not get me a good office on Glasgow and Ayr Railway, he could do so in some house in Manchester. – [45] Went to my Latin lesson. Caught a severe cold with going without drawers. O the failures of these ill-trained bodies of ours.

SATURDAY AUG 19 [*August 21st*] – With what intense interest I have read two beautiful extracts from Miss Martineau's book on the Holy Land! Travels always please me, but this delightfully told account of a sojourn in the most remarkable spot in the world in its historic associations, fascinated me in an uncommon degree. And not the least element of the absorbing influence this book has over me, arises from my having been trained from my early youth to the reading of the Scriptures – When very young my mother accustomed me to read a portion, chiefly of the New Testament, to her every day – I delighted, too, – wild wanderer as I was in other respects – I loved to accompany her to the Wesleyan chapel – I was a Sunday Scholar, too, and, altogether, the lessons I received at school – my poor mother's teaching – the hints dropt from the services at chapel infused a deeper tinge of religious feeling into my natural love for all that is holy in Spirit and for all the forms and ordinances of religion. – That poor mother of mine that struggled in poverty and sickness, and obscurity, to teach her little [46] wild colt of a lad to read in the Scriptures has tended more than all things to make me a bible-lover and a god-lover, and a God-fearer to the day of my death! – And now I never meet with a book explanatory of that noble one, and I never read anything allusive to that contemplative oriental land, the history, and biographies of which so wrought upon my youthful mind, but I read it eagerly and wish to possess it.

I met with a young man a printer who first completed his apprenticeship in one of the offices in the town, and who is now, like myself, out of employment – He seems to me a helpless, inexperienced driveller – I talked with him about the prospects of workmen in our trade, and such like things till the gloom of his own cowardly faithlessness began to infect my own mind.

[47] *Waugh then reflects on his physical weaknesses, citing Dr. Johnson, Burns and Carlyle as examples of 'mens sana in corpore sano' in marked contrast to himself.*

[48] **SATURDAY AUG 22** – My mind confused today – As I crost the fields at noon, I passed near where a party of brutal vagabonds lay drinking under a hedge and, it being time of Divine Service, they were supplied with drink from a neighbouring Ale-House, thus avoiding the consequences of a visit from the police – I overheard conversations that made my soul sicken at the thought of man –

MONDAY AUG 23 – [*More reflections on his relationship with God 'as I lay in Foxholes wood at noon' take up much of this entry* [48, 49], *then ...*]

[50] John Chadwick met me in the street and after talking with me a few minutes respecting the appearance of the river in former times,

the history of the town, and such like matters, he inquired if I was a native of the town and said he had often noticed me about Holden's shop and admired my clean sober-looking appearance – He wondered that Holden did not prefer one such as he took me to be about his business before any kind of stranger that he could get. – He was still more astonished to find that I was the son of that quondam shoemaker with whom his brother William – now one of the magistrates – kept a bachelor's house for sometime in their wild youth. – he said he could now perceive the unmistakable [sic] marks of our family likeness in my face and figure very plainly – went to my Latin Lesson – Progressing in it a little more hopefully.

TUESDAY AUG 25 [*24th*] – ... [51] Saw 2 remarkable pictures today in Entwisle's collection[4] – One a fine portrait of 'Cromwell' and the other 'The Burial of Christ' a painting so natural and impressive that it bound me to the spot.

WEDNESDAY AUG 31 [*September 1st*] I lay in bed late this morning wearied in body though less disturbed in mind than might be expected from the unpropitious aspect of my affairs. My wife and me had just one halfpenny between us, and we knew not where the next meal was to come from; and expected every day to be turned out of my lodgings. – Winter coming with every promise of uncommon severity, and my trade in a very depressed condition – But what grieved me most was the money I owed; without present chance of repayment. –

I found 2 vols of 'Land o Burns' at 'Sally's' today – I never turn from the stream of men and books that chance has thrown in my way to pore over life and works of Burns again but I feel instantly revived and inflamed with emulation of the startling truth and nobleness of his character.

[52] **SATURDAY, SEP 3** [*4th*] – I find all the 'proud helpers' whom I have depended on too foolishly and confidently have failed and I begin to think of the proverb 'God helps them that help themselves.'

MONDAY, SEP. 6 – I am so confused and depressed by the infernal concatenation of miseries that beset me just now that I feel as if I was

---

[4] The Entwisle's (aka Entwistle) were owners of Foxholes where Aunt Sally (Sarah Wood), who plays a major part in this narrative, was a lodge-keeper.

hopelessly hell-doomed – so little is there in life worth living for, that death [*deletion*] unembittered by the gall of dependence on this brutal world 'is a consummation devoutly to be wished' – [*Here there is a longer deletion*] – ignorant girl, who has been ruined by a mother coarser and ignoranter than herself. – she has been so petted and waited upon, and strengthened in dawdling helplessness and [*deletion*] that there is no living near her in anything like order or cleanliness or peace of mind. – but I must 'bide my time', and bite my lips, and make the best I can of what seems to my poor blind thoughts, a miserably bad bargain. – [*More self deprecation follows ...*]

[53] **FRIDAY SEPTEMBER 10TH** – I just now think of a remarkable saying of the poet Grays [*sic*] which Burns quotes in one of his letters saying that a half a word noted down at or near the spot is worth a cartload of recollection. I have felt this so frequently and forcibly and have so often desired a moment's opportunity to chronicle a thought when I could not get a moment's opportunity and have squandered so much true pleasure and benefit by neglecting to catch them and express them in writing even when I might have done so, that I feel more determined than ever to keep my diary more strictly than heretofore. Writing is such an inexpressible delight to me. It enhances every other joy that visits me, and it soothes every sorrow of my heart to write. – I am ambitious to excel in writing – It is impossible to write well without thought and feeling. – Yesterday I came to Manchester by the noon train to see Sowler the proprietor of the <u>Courier</u> newspaper. He had promised to give me 2 days employment a week in his printing office. My heart saddened as I saw the moors and fells of Blackstone Edge recede and the [54] <u>clangor</u> [*sic*] and corruption of this great sooty city advance upon us. Dr. Coates had come by the train and hailed me as I walked from the station. He enquired whither I was bound, and on my telling him I was going to compose a few 'stickfulls' of Tory type for Sowler, he said 'Tell Sowler his <u>Courier</u> is the greatest blackguard in England – and I thought myself it was a rare specimen of the genus humbug. – but then I must live and I have nothing for it but my labour. – tis for the bare life – 'Tis for the regainment of some of that peace of mind which I have lost by thoughtlessly getting into debt that I am struggling just now, otherwise I have no affection for such an employment. – However, off I set to see if I could be allowed to 'leg up' about a column of 'Minton' this afternoon for bread and cheese. – I went into Sowler's shop – Holden, who had

spoken to Sowler on the subject, had desired me to see Sowler, and to confer with him on the subject, and with no other person. – When I inquired for him, a little buff faced woman, who looked as if she had soot in the creases of her visage came up to me with a busy prompt air and asked if I wished to see him particularly, and on business. – I did – She seemed unwilling or afraid to tell him – he was engaged and I had better wait and [55] see his son. – I said no more, but took up a book from the counter and read determined not to be ridded till he could be seen – In a few minutes, the door of the inner office opened and she ushered me into the den of this grandiloquent spectacled, conservative bullock. There stood the bashan of the Courier – a bluff-bodied, bald-headed man with a red nose and surly self-important countenance! – I marked the big littleness expressed in his way of holding his lumpish face – I thought that 'Jack Falstaff' would have looked o' this fashion if he had enacted Joshua commanding the sun to stand still – I prayed for a painter! – But it was no use. He was 'alone in his glory', and the world lost a picture that would have made thousands blush for the absurdity of humanity, and forswear all kinds of pitiful pomp, and turn true men, thenceforward for ever. – I accosted him with my message, which he rudely interrupted with 'Who?' 'What?' 'Speak up!' – 'Go in there.' 'Well, what is it?' – I instantly raised my voice to an alarming pitch, and kept it up till I had finished my message – 'O, why could not you tell my son that?' – [56] 'Stay where you are.' He returned with his son, a good-looking and a better tempered person than his august fool of a father. He told me that they had not a vacancy for full employment at present, but they could give me 2 days a week, which would enable me to look out. He then handed me over to the foreman, who took me up to the Office, gave me a pair of 'Minton Cases', and copy. I set a 'long take' of disgusting police news, and accounts of murders and robberies, until my heart grew unconsciously melancholy and despondent. I was grieving too for the loss of the green fields, and this great black city, full of rushing to and fro, and discordant tumults was somehow, as all city life is, repulsive to my feelings. – However, I determined to make the best of it until I could amend my condition – At noon, I went into a cook's shop and dined heartily. – I took up the Guardian, and read Dickens's sketch of Tootle the stoker,[5] – a picture so graphically true and

---

[5]   From the currently publishing *Dombey and Son*.

humorous that I am sure it must have aided my digestion exceedingly by the silent roar of laughter it roused up in the dormant recesses of my heart. – I returned [57] to the office. – it was the day before publication. – Within was heard but the ticking of types in the 'composing stick' of the types, and the tapping of their snuff boxes as they whispered their jokes and exchanged pinches of snuff with one another. The noise of the 'devils' running to and fro with 'copy' and 'proof' and 'comps' emptying their sticks of 'matter' and now and then some jaded letterless wight, after a long and fruitless search for hoarded 'soils' for the want of which he could not proceed with his copy, would howl out with indignant determination to terrify the hiders into a revelation of their concealed treasure – 'Has any gentleman got any himperial capital h's in his <u>pocket</u> – I can't set without letters' – Then another breaks through the low irreverent whispers of these beery pickers up of 'nonpareil' with 'who has number 15 of the 'Feed', or the 'devil' rushes in again shouting out 'Here's the 'Deaths and Marriages' with a handful of 'Murders' and 'Markets'. What a miniature of human life! After I left the office I went to sup, and smoke and sleep with 'Maddle'. The water playing in and out of my boots like 'Pump-suckers'. – Had to lounge hungrily around Manchester reading in windows and snuffing the wind about cook's shops, and longing [58] for a brown crust and a green field till 4 o'clock p.m. at which time they pay at the Courier office – I lost no time in quitting by the train this hell-hole of earth creeping bargainers and schemers – was so heartily disgusted with [*gap in writing*] deportment that I secretly resolved to have as little communion as possible.

It is at this point that Waugh gained his new position as Assistant Secretary of the Lancashire Public Schools Association, though no direct reference is made to it in the diary. September 15th 1848 (see p. 57) is recorded as the anniversary of the appointment.

WEDNESDAY SEPT. 15TH – I have felt uncommonly 'wooden' in my new vacation today and depressed by the fear of not satisfying those who employ me. I am inwardly mourning, too, about my neglect of rhyme. I went into a printing office to enquire about circular printing for the Association and found the pressmen at work on a new volume of poetry by Charles Swaine [*sic*] – my heart bounded with emulation and cheer, at the sight. – I could not light the gas in the office. [*Sentence erased*] – A pint and a pipe with a 'pup'.

MONDAY OCT. 4ᵀᴴ – Walked away from the old farmhouse this morning to meet the seven o'clock train at Rochdale – Laden with a heavy heart. – My wife is, at once, a pleasure, a revelation, a mystery and a misery! – She is an unhappiness and an hindrance in all worldly affairs, true. But for what wise spiritual purposes she has been sent to me I know not, but I do believe for the best. – the Rev. W. Smith, my Latin teacher [59] called at the office to see me. – He took me aside and gave me some wholesome advice in such a kindly and earnest tone that my attachment to him has been strengthened ever since.

FRIDAY OCT. 8ᵀᴴ. – This town would be a complete hell of soot and stench but that it is drenched by incessant rain and wrapt in a succession of thick fogs, which, together with the 'inhuman dearth' of the fair array of [*deletion*] natural beauty makes it the most infernal cluster of human habitation on earth. Soaked to the skin and dried on the back thrice today. – Too poor to buy a second-hand cotton umbrella. – Yet I have borrowed and paid as much for breaking and losing them within these few weeks as would buy half a dozen. – Walking close to the shops in Oldham Street today to avoid the rain a mischievous imp of a nail caught the tail of my coat – my only one – that not long since cost, but no matter, for, worse than all, it is not yet paid for. – Oh, the damned misery of debt – it was invented by the devil, however, as I was saying, this devil of a nail caught the tail, and ripped it up to – up to my heart's content, as the saying is – one of my laps had increased its longitude most unbecomingly and dangled in melancholy apathy to the ground, leaving a large piece of coarse grey tailor's padding or wadding exposed to the view – I tucked up my tail among a host of pretty titterers, and shoving the [60] ruins ['*of my copy*' *inserted*] into my still uninjured pocket, that looked as lonely as a new made widow, I 'went on my way and was no more seen' – It has been a day full of funny disasters. – But what

> 'The best laid schemes of mice and men
>   Aft gang agley
> And here is naught but care and pain
>   For promised joy.'

I feel almost ashamed of quoting such a piece for such a purpose! – Read a chapter of Thomas a Kempis – Listened to evening service in Holy Trinity Church.

SUNDAY OCT 10TH – I rose out of bed at nine this morning – I was so disturbed by the careless, lazy, irreverent manner in which my wife lolls away the beautiful Sabbath that my peace was murdered outright. – What an evidence of weakness in me! – I did nothing but mope about the fields and hedges in the rain, saunter into the house and out of the house, and round about the house melancholily sick at heart, and unable to find rest for my unhappy spirit anywhere. – I transcribed a chapter of Thomas a Kempis at night, went through the curst infliction of writing an explanatory letter to an impatient creditor, and went to bed ill satisfied with myself and everything about me.

[61] **TUESDAY OCT 12TH**. – Ill in body and weary in mind. – Tribulation and sorrow – That shock on Sunday afternoon agitates me yet. – My poor wife! – If ever I speak unkindly to her, it is a grievous sin against my own heart. – I pray God that I may ever behave gently and forbearingly towards my own wife. –

WEDNESDAY 13TH. – Went to Rochdale in the evening. – Slept at Peanock. –

THURSDAY 14TH. – Delayed in Rochdale till the noon train. – I met Miss Osborne at the station. Manchester at 10 min. to 1 – Pretty little child with its mother in the carriage. – Read 10th and 11th of Job.

During this period Waugh began to attend Christian services more regularly, chiefly attending Holy Trinity Church (Littleborough Parish Church) but also services at Grosvenor Street Baptist Chapel. His diary gives detailed accounts of some of the sermons he heard. The places where he worshipped are recorded below but the sermons are not.

SUNDAY OCT 24TH. – Went to Holy Trinity Church in the morning ...

In the evening I went to Grosvenor Street Baptist Chapel, where I listened to a beautiful and impressive sermon by David Rhys Stevens ...

[62] **SUNDAY OCT. 30TH**. [*31st*] – D. R. Steven's chapel ... [63] Holy Trinity Church.

THURSDAY NOV. 4TH. – I resolved to begin immediately at the simple elements of Arithmetic and proceed steadily through the different department [*sic*] of mathematical knowledge till I have mastered the most abstruse. – I seldom grieve for the emptiness of my pockets except when I meet with books, teachers and pictures.

There then follows a list of Chinese proverbs.

FRIDAY NOV. 5TH. – Letter from Chas. Reddish, Leader of the Roscoe Club, Liverpool and from H. Walker [?] Lucas Esq. of Lyme House Prescot, Jas. Wescoe of Heywood, Se. M. Trust. – Two hours in Arithmetic!

[64] **SATURDAY NOVEMBER 6TH.** – Letters from Latham of Lancaster and Friend Drewry of Fleetwood. – The miseries of servitude; and the double distilled misery of ignorance!

More self recrimination follows, including an unfinished poem.

[65] Went to David Rhys Stephen's Bible Class this evening ...

SUNDAY NOV 7TH.

> The Sabbath-day is breaking
> With its divine calm
> In gentle accents speaking
> Words of holy balm.
>
> Like an angel preaching
> Against this earthly strife,
> It moves by winsome teaching
> To the better life.
>
> And weary hearts and lorn,
> Sin and sorrow-riven
> The beauty of this morn
> Woos again for heaven.
>
> Day of heavenly rest
> To this sin sick sod,
> Leading souls unblest
> Back again to God.

I went to Holy Trinity Church at Morning Service – 34, 35, 36, Psalm – 11 Prov. – 23rd Luke – I was, as I oft have been, disgusted by the false whining tone in which the ministers, especially one, delivered his sermon and read the beautiful service of the Church. – This way of speaking and reading is a common desecration of the services of Religion and chiefly in the Churches of the Establishment. – There is more that is absolutely ridiculous than any way impressive in this assumption of a most comical and inhuman gesture and tone whenever [66] they enter on the performance of what ought to be done in the most earnest [?] and reverential manner – 'with heart and souls [*sic*] and strength'. – And these very men, that 'counterfeit humanity so abominably' in the fulfilment of the greatest office which can engage the powers of man, – when they come down from the rostrum and doff the surplice will speak to you with ten-fold the grace and force about any two penny affair, because they unconsciously speak naturally 'from the fullness of the heart', and with unassumed earnestness respecting it. Went to David Rhys Stephen's chapel at night with my wife.

> Here's to faith and ruth
> The wide world around
> Here's to God-like truth
> Wherever it is found.
>
> Here's to all truth-seekers
> Seeking as they ought
> Here's to all truth speakers,
> Speaking, dreading nought.

There follows an extended account of the sermon.

[68] **MONDAY, NOV. 7TH** [*8th*] – M.A. very low-spirited and myself unhappy on her account – unhappy for my own failings – coming to dinner in the afternoon, I found that she had left, and gone home to Rochdale, in a melancholy mood – God help us both!

TUESDAY NOV. 8TH. [*9th*] – Wrote to my brother. Wrote to Sally

———

> I hearken for the feet
> Once music in my ears,
> I look in every face,
> Alas! I see not hers.

[69] **WEDNESDAY, NOV. 9TH**. [*10th*] – Wrote to Charles Howarth and John Crossley. – O my poor wife! [*'wife' is actually crossed out*]

THURSDAY, NOV. 11TH. – Went to Holy Trinity Church, at night Service – Read the Book of Ecclesiastes.

Another melancholy poem follows and his dejected mood is continued in the next entry made a week later on the 18th of November.

[70] **FRIDAY, NOV. 19TH 1847.** – Wrote to Charles Howarth and to John Crossley of Rochdale; and to Thomas Lamb of Wakefield – Late at the offices tonight – Meeting of the Committee.

SATURDAY. NOV. 20TH. 1847 – Hobbled for cash tonight. – Hardly know how to make ends meet – Must eat my library. – Immortal bard, befriend me! – Shakespeare farewell!

An attempt at a poem follows.

[71] **SUNDAY, NOV. 21ST** Holy Trinity Church, morning Service preaching on St. Mark.
   David Rhys Stevens Church in the evening. Wrote to Buckley, Peanock, Rochdale.

MONDAY, NOVEMBER 22ND Received letters from Charles Howarth, Martin Brown and Calderwood of Liverpool. Went to Emerson's lecture on 'Reading'. – I felt so inspired by the whole tone of this man's thoughts, and the beauty and force of his language – nay I felt so inflamed with love for this lofty minded [*'man' inserted*], gentleman and scholar that I could have wept like a child when I began to think how soon he would leave this country and perhaps be 'no more seen' here again – not every man I meet moves me thus! – That miserable drawler in the pontificals on Sunday moved me 'tis true – but after a very different fashion to this! – I watched Emerson as he walked away with Mr. Ireland, and I thought of the passage 'How beautiful are the feet of those that preach the gospel of peace.' – My heart is with that man to its last beat.

TUESDAY NOVEMBER 23RD 1847 – Sick and unhappy from head to foot, from the perpetual internal conflict between [*word deleted*] and duty. – Domestic grievances. The evening of the Provisional Committee Meeting. – Wrote to Charles Howarth of Rochdale, an humble honest man –

'A king of men, for a'that.' –

[72] I can feel Emerson's lecture taking root in my mind and whole demeanor [*sic*] as I walk about in the streets thinking of man, of God and my relations with these. – Emerson is turning upside down some of my schemes – and remodelling my plans of life! – he has indeed given me great hints both in his books and in his lectures, which my memory will linger o'er as long as I live! –

WEDNESDAY NOV. 24TH – My head and my heart are disturbed this morning all for the sake of Mary Ann. – My own wife! – May the God that made us keep us in love and in honour to the end of our lives. – lie down in our graves at last. How much forgiveness I need for the bitterness of this unruly tongue! O that my wife would be my one true friend, and help me and guide me, and love me, and forgive me! – God and my wife! – my heart and life is theirs! –

THURSDAY, NOV. 25TH. Wrote to Thomas Lamb of Wakefield – Resolved to commence my Latin exercises again tomorrow, and continue them daily –

Rhyming a little –

> 'Rude and rough
> But crooning to a body's 'sel'
> Does well enough'

[73] **FRIDAY, NOV. 24TH** [*26th*] – Holden shouted to me today and inquired what business I was engaged in. – Engaged at the Meeting of the Sub-Committee tonight. – Horace Mann's Educational Report – Anxious about lecture and a world of other more heart-fretting matters than that. – I had resolved to commence a review of my Latin today. – Here I am late at night and it has not been looked at yet – I am heartily sick of procrastination – but there is only half a wick of candle in the house, I have not a copper, the shops are all closed, and the folks are asleep and so will I be soon. – Good night Cesar [*sic*]!

SATURDAY NOV. 27TH. – Mr S advised me in writing not to make use of words that were not in the English language, and then shewed his ignorance by mentioning one – the word 'allusive', which he said was not in the dictionary – An hour with my Latin grammar – wrote to John Crossley of Rochdale – Reading epistle to the Galatians. – The 'Public School Association' slackens its operations, and I must look out – Its purposes are not pursued with spirit and liberality of expenditure, – it is cramped by little carefulnesses in the outlay and its measures are [74] not large and prompt enough. – I took the Legend of Montrose out of the library close by, and sat by the fireside surrounded by Highland chiefs and bare-legged caterans and Pipers while in the room close to me our Welsh landlord and his wife were jabbering in Welsh like monkeys in a coconut tree.

SUNDAY NOVEMBER 28TH. – Missed Church this forenoon and solaced my mortification with Scott's Legend of Montrose. – finished the story and sat by the fire till evening musing on the past, the present and the future. – wove about a foot of limping rhyme. – went to David Rhys Steven's chapel, and heard to my disappointment an entirely theological sermon on the Godhead of Christ – a doctrine of which I am not profoundly convinced according to his notions. – There is something grand in the conception for all that. – He used bitter words against the Unitarians.

MONDAY NOVR. 29TH. Went to Emerson's lecture on the Superlative in Manners and Literature – Profound and scholarly – Language the most beautiful and terse lighted up by sentiments full of nobleness – remarkable quotations from the Persian of Hafi. – [75] Wrote to my mother and wrote a Latin exercise.

TUESDAY NOV. 30TH. – An uncommonly large and animated meeting of the Association at the offices this evening [*Deletions*] spurred me on to greater exertions in the pursuit of literature. [*Deletions*].

WEDNESDAY DEC. 1ST. 1847 – Wrote to J. B. Stephens of Rochdale, accompanied by a parcel of Pamphlets of the Educational Plan of the Association. – Read notes of Emerson's Lectures in the Guardian newspaper. – Preparing letter for the Guardian – Latin exercise. – I went to the Conversazione at the Salford Literary and Mechanical Institution. – The room was filled and Dr. Watts gave a lucid explanation of the details of the Plan published by the Association and was followed by Mr. Lucas in a neat speech. – The plan is an excellent one and that makes the surest ground of its success. But its projectors have not that species of energy which can talk [*blotted*] notability. – There is a timidity about their measures that retards its progress. – but, in spite of all that, there is such worth in the principles of the scheme as will warrant its warm reception among the whole people.

[76] **THURSDAY DEC. 2ND.** Wrote to Charles Howarth of Rochdale. – my stomach turned inside out by the unwomanly and [*word smudged*] conduct of mon femme [*sic*]. Indignant at the senseless growls from sectarian ministers on all sides at the Athenaum – so dulled by a headache that I have no power to think or desire to read. – Preparing every day to set soundly to study.

FRIDAY 3RD. Painful Headache – Read a few pages of Horace Mann's Educational Tour – wrote letter for the Guardian – An hour's Latin. – A flimsy way of wearing out ones period of existence. – I do nothing.

SATURDAY, DEC 4TH. – Wrote verses to Julia Ashton. – Reading 'Ivanhoe' in a happy hour. Stretched on three chairs before the fire, listening to the singing of an iron tea-kettle.

SUNDAY DEC 5TH. – Holy Trinity Church, at Morning Church – The rotten talk of the Preacher – Rhys Stevens Chapel in the evening.

MONDAY DEC 6. – Reading 'Ivanhoe' – intensely interested in this wonderful novel. – Received a letter from 'Robin' the 'cowlad' at the 'Peanock', containing an account [77] of the good-will and the conditions of all my friends in that beloved lonely nook where I have spent so many delightful hours more beautiful now in remembrance even than they were then in reality. – 'Robin's' letter that my valued friend 'Captain' the sheep-cur had gotten better of his lameness, and that 'th'Hollingworth lodge were quite full o'waytur.'

SUNDAY, DEC 7 – Reading 'Ivanhoe' – Received a letter from my mother. – My mind confused with a host of distracting considerations, among which the thought that time is flitting away and I am doing very little for my mental and moral nature is one of the foremost thoughts of my mind.

WEDNESDAY DEC 8 [?] – Reading 'Ivanhoe' – wrote to 'Robin' and to Charles Howarth.

THURSDAY, DEC. 9. [?] – I am oppressed by a saddening consciousness of the unlingering haste with which life flies away, and the tardiness of my advancement towards that nobler condition of body and soul that shines before my mind's eye continually and makes me miserable at heart – O for fire and energy – Resolved

[78, 79] *There follows the outline of a poem with many deletions and another complaint about his lack of moral value.*

SUNDAY DEC 12 – Holy Trinity Church, Morning and Evening Service.

MONDAY DEC. 13. Tales of the Crusades. – the Betrothed. – When I look back upon the day I am ashamed.

TUESDAY, DEC 14. – Rose a little earlier – I have neglected my Latin these few days past. I will begin it this evening again.

WEDNESDAY, DEC 15. – Latin in the shade – and partly asleep, and I half-dead with [*deletion*].

[80] **THURSDAY, DEC 16TH.** – Reading the 'Betrothed' –Writing letter on the Educational Plan to the Preston Guardian. –

> Late one night I sat
> In my lonely room
> All around one was
> Silent as the tomb
>
> Save the rattling sound
> Of some prowling mouse
> And the kitchen clock
> Ticking in the house.
>
> Now thought is the hour,
> Now's the happy time
> I will try my power
> At a spell of rhyme.
>
> I pored on a while
> But no more did know
> What to write about
> Than the dead below.
>
> Dull as any lead
> Sleepy was my look
> As I scratched my head
> O'er the empty book.

'The devil's thrown his club
Over me,' I said,
Then threw down my pen
And ran up to bed.

FRIDAY DEC 17TH – Writing for Newspaper – Writing report of Conversazione at Salford Mechanics' Institutes.

SATURDAY DEC 18 – Concert – Tempestuous entertainment 'The Shamrock, the Rose and the Thistle' or the National Songs of England Scotland and Ireland. – 'The lads of the village' –

[81] *On this page there are quotations from the songs – including Burns and Scottish dialect.*

[82] **SUNDAY DEC 19** – Holy Trinity Church – Anthem 'O thou that tellest good tidings to Zion' – Sermon hissing hot with hell and damnation. The whole church smelt of sulphur and the lights burn blue.

MONDAY 20 – An hours Arithmetic. – Count Robert of Paris – Channings Pamphlet in defence of Unitarianism. –

There follows a long underlining and then:

Went to Rochdale on Christmas Eve. – Slept at Foxholes. – A disagreeable spot to me. Spent the forenoon of Christmas day in a ramble with John Stephens, and the remainder of the day at Mrs Stephen's house. – Slept at Foxholes again. – During the day disgusting quarrels had occurred between my wife, her brother, her aunt and mother – I was miserably disturbed when I heard of it, and for many a day after. – I have hoped to wean her away from connections that do her no good – from ignorance and brutality and blackguardism – but I have not done so yet. – I am grieved and disgusted by these things, and with myself too, for they make me unkind and rude to every-body about me. –

83 **SUNDAY 26** – I walked with Crossley across the moors to 'Blue Pots Spring'. – The air was bitter cold but these heathery hills are beautiful in all seasons of the year – and the little streams that run down the lovely glens between seemed livelier and lovelier even than when the green leaves of summer canopied them, and the bright green blae-berry

bush and the graceful lady-bracken dipt their waters as they [*deletion*] and rambled away through the solitary moorland haunts – the thrush [?] and the throstle mimicked their song. –

Conversation on the charms of Scottish Minstrelsy – Mary Morrison – 'A man's a man for a' that – Highland Mary – The Jolly Beggar – Auld Lang Syne – Bruce's address. – St. Stephen's church at night Lewis's preached [*sic*] on the beautiful narrative of Jacob's visit to his son Joseph at the court of Pharaoh–. An hour with John Irvine.

–The day was nearly done and I walked with unwilling footsteps towards my roosting place, because I do not like the doings there, and cannot feel at home.

84 **MONDAY 27TH** Took the noon train for Manchester, my heart burthened with melancholy luggage – Meeting of the Executive Committee at night.

A week of melancholy musings

[84] **TUESDAY JANUARY 4TH.** – I am determined to live a better life than I have done till now and I will begin immediately, in the first place, by rising earlier in a morning, and eating nothing after seven o'clock in the evening. – I will pay strict attention to a daily examination of my resolutions, and the progress I make in the performance of them.

Went to see an Esquimaux and his wife Uckalue, he brought from devil's Strait by Captain Parker last month in a whaler. The expression of their countenances was pleasing, and the female had an unassuming modesty in her face and manner that would put to shame many of the civilized ladies that laughed senselessly at this unassuming wild beauty in her seal skin hood and kirtle.

[85, 86] *The next two pages are taken up with gloomy introspection and musing on his relationship with God.*

[87] **THURSDAY, 6TH JANUARY.** – The fog so dense and black that the shops and offices throughout the town were lighted up the whole day. I had a dreadful fit of thirsting in the night-time, followed by great feverishness. – To my great relief, however, in about two hours after I broke into a sweat and fell soundly asleep.

FRIDAY 7TH – Letters from Thomas Lamb of Wakefield – from Mr. Lucas of Highhurst – Daly of Rochdale and John Bent. – Meeting of the executive Committee in the Evening – High time for me to study my lecture at the People's Institute! – Letters from Jonathan Binns of Lancaster and Rev Peter Kaye, Roman Catholic Priest of Blackburn.

MONDAY 17TH JANY 1848 – Sat in Entwistle Lodge till noon, my heart disturbed in me with present discomfort and future bodings – O this unhappy contract!

THURSDAY 20TH JANY 1848 – One uneasiness follows another like the waves of the sea.

[88] Beware of familiarity! It cheapens a man and breeds disgust, especially in shallower minds. 'Do unto others as you would that others

should do unto you.' Live like God! – ['*Never demean thyself*' inserted] but humble thy condition of life, whatever it may be. –

I never felt so down-hearted and soiled a thing in my life as now. My marriage has torn my wife and me asunder instead of knitting us closer to one another. – every day almost every [*sic*] we do seems to hurry us on to some miserable close of this unhappy course of living. – Lovelessness between us every day, and dislike increases – I am very unhappy! I feel less sensitive, and more brutal than I used to do, and the consciousness of this gives me no peace … [*More introspection follows.*]

[89] Last Wednesday night my wife got up about one in the morning, and dressed herself, and went into the silent streets. – The night was black dark and a heavy shower of rain was falling. – I dressed myself and followed to seek for her with a heart as heavy as lead. She makes me thoroughly miserable. If there be any good in unhappiness few men are more blessedly endowed than I am. There is no unity of character and aim between us, and she has neither education nor help in her, and what is worse, she seems to have no wish for either – She is the spoiled child too of a most coarse and ignorant mother. – She is neglectful and pettish and fretful every hour. The day is eaten up with coarse cavils that make me disgusted and distrest, by night and by day, both for myself and for her. If there was any chance of improvement for her and for me by living together I should be happy to think of it, but every change up to this has been for the worst. She has been dandled and petted and waited upon by female relatives who have neither natural sense, manners nor discretion, that now when she comes to have to wait upon herself, let alone having [90] a house to attend to, she is helpless as an infant, and sluttish and miserable and makes me so too – Everything is in confusion and dirty – a thing which disgusts me exceedingly, who have been born and bred up by one of the poorest, and withal one of the cleanest and most industrious women in the land. – I am thoroughly sick of helplessness and petty repinings and filth. –

SATURDAY NIGHT, 15TH APRIL 1848 – I am uncommonly comfortable tonight. I am revelling in the luxury of a three-legged deal table, without paint, and four chairs, the first articles of furniture which have graced our dwelling here. – We have lived in this house more than three months, our only seats two deal drawers pulled out of a fixture cupboard in the wall, our only piece of furniture of any kind, a flimsy little, dirty, worm-eaten deal table which my wife had borrowed from the wife of a journeyman stone-mason in the neighbourhood, and so small and thin that a decent-sized plate, and a penn'orth of onions almost put the surface of it out of sight, and the weight of a thrupenny brown loaf and a quartern of cheese (with one of my [91] elbows to boot) made it quiver ominously – My wife mended the children's frocks for the loan of that spider-limbed table ...

There follows almost a page of whimsical musings about this deal table.

I have neglected my diary now about three months. – I now resume it with pleasure. – Writing soothes my sorrows and increases my pleasures. It is never far from my thoughts.

[92] **SUNDAY 16ᵀᴴ APRIL 1848.** – Finished Mavor's [?] English History. Began to read Milton's 'Ekonoklastes' or 'The Image Breaker'. – Took a short walk in the fields after dinner. – Brought a handfull [*sic*] of graceful green things from the hedge-side whose names I did not know. I put them in a glass bottle of water, and put on the table with twopennyworth of daisy roots that I bought last night . – Their beauty made me glad. – I went to church at night. The Evening Psalms for the day, beginning 'God standeth in the congregation of princes: he is a Judge among gods.

How long will ye give wrong judgements and accept the persons of the ungodly?

Defend the poor and fatherless: see that such as are in need and necessity have right.

Deliver the outcast and poor: save them from the hand of the ungodly.

They will not learn or understand but walk on still in darkness: all the foundations of the earth are out of course – etc.

These psalms struck me from their application to the events of the times.

[93] **MONDAY, 17 APRIL** – Read a few pages of the 'Ekonaklastes' and the 7ᵗʰ and 8ᵗʰ chapters of St. Matthew. – The night beautifully still and balmy. The full moon shines, and straggling snowy clouds are sailing eastward over the blue heavens. – How strange and strong the sympathy between external nature and the heart of man! –

TUESDAY 18 APRIL 1848. – Went at night to hear Henry Vincent's third lecture on 'Cromwell and the Commonwealth' – While I listened to his portraiture of the noble band of souls who confronted and crushed the despotic tyrant who set his infamous will in array against the liberties and lives of the people who so long and bitterly suffered under his damnable domination I felt myself nobly moved with a sense of the dignity and power of right principles in man's nature ...

Waugh continues in this vein for some time.

[94] **SATURDAY NIGHT, 22ND APRIL, 1848** I feel so fatigued by such exertion and a succession of severe colds to boot that I have no spirit for thinking or writing or speaking, and, here I have been sitting these two hours, turning and twisting from one side of my chair to the other, misery in every position, tired of sitting up, sick of gazing about me, weary of walking and afraid to go to bed because I know beforehand I cannot sleep there. The last miserable remnant of the fire too is lingering languidly in the centre of four or five moderate-fired cinders, amid a handfull [*sic*] of spiritless ashes, – a most melancholy picture of decline and desolation, and, but for a two-penny 'posie' which I bought and brought up from the town, the whole house looks a desert and dispirited look. [*sic*] ...

More melancholy reflections continue through this page, through page 95, and in the entry for Sunday 23 April on page 96. The writing at this point becomes much neater.

[96] **WEDNESDAY 26TH APRIL 1848.** Walked up Cheetham Hill Road. Pleasant and refreshing to me coming out of the heart of Manchester! I have often remarked what a beneficial alteration a new and natural scene is to my mind especially after treading the gin horse routine of mere earth-grubbing business awhile in the fume and riot of such a town as this. Who shall say that external nature has not wise hints to give us as well as reviving balm? – I believe Wordsworth's theory that there is boundless provision made by the Creator in external nature for the education of man.

> 'One impulse from a vernal wood
>   May teach thee more of man,
> Of moral evil and of good
>   Than all the sages can.'

I went into the new Catholic Church at Cheetham Hill.[1] – Sacred music always affects me sacredly. – I seldom go into a place of worship of any kind that I am not struck with the thought that men are far more absorbed with the pleasures and cares of this life than they have been at some [97] periods of the world's history. There is no earnestness in the devotion of the times, no truth in the legislation. Men are clever makers and determined winners of this world's goods, but 'God is not in all their thoughts.' I too am of the number of those who are apt to forget that divine being 'whose service is perfect freedom', but it never was love of pelf that made me forget him, I can say truly. My heart and head are busy tonight preparing weft and warp for weaving a new and better web of life than I have ever manufactured before. I hope and pray that I may have the resolution to keep my looms going right till the piece is 'downed' and that my work may gain the approval of the master 'looker' when it is carried home.[2]

My mother's anecdote of her childish interpretation of the sentence 'Blessed are the peacemakers, for they shall inherit the kingdom of heaven'. She translated it 'piece-maker' and looked on her father's household as registered in heaven because they were all employed in making flannel pieces for the market in Rochdale.

THURSDAY 27TH APRIL 1848. – Canvassing for signatures to the Petition. – I am very unwell or else the continual succession of disputation and explanation which this piece of business enforces upon me, and the strange variety of characters it brings me in contact with is both [98] amusing and very instructive to me.

Further resolutions to improve follow.

SATURDAY 29TH APRIL 1848. A jovial hour with 'Old Uncle Jem'.[3]

'Tempest' at the Theatre Royal.

SUNDAY 30TH APRIL 1848 Felt uncommonly ill and weak and lay in bed late. Took a delightful with [*sic*] Mary Ann in the evening past the Independent College and towards Withington.

---

[1] Opened 3rd August 1847, Axon 1886.
[2] A familiar metaphor with Lancashire writers.
[3] The first reference to the bookseller James Weatherley, the bookseller who figures prominently in the diary.

MONDAY 1ST MAY 1848. Went to Rochdale in the evening in company with my wife. – Deeply grieved at heart and full of unhappy reflections. 'Quid dejectis anima mea? Spere in Deo quoniam ad huius confitator illis. Subitare multus mei'.

TUESDAY 2ND MAY 1848 – Started from Rochdale by the Special Train at 51 [?] m past 10. – Ran the distance in 20 min. – Went to Vincent's last lecture on 'Cromwell and the Commonwealth.' – a spirit-stirring subject! – [99] A glorious page of English History! What a band of noble men God grouped together here. It makes me mournful to feel the immeasurable difference between such hearts as these and mine.

Rd. Gardner, M.P. for Leicester called at the office to-day and promised to continue his letters in the Manchester Guardian in defence of the 'Plan of Secular Education' – Committee Meeting in the evening. – Received a letter from Mr. Lucas of Ben Rhydding. –

Resolved to live to God and be no more the slave of sin and fools.

The entry for Wednesday 3rd of May 1848 is an undecipherable poem beginning 'Rosy May is here again, with its flowery sheen'.

[100] **THURSDAY 4 MAY.** Ill, ill from head to foot inside. My left breast particularly affected. I feel confused and unable to read or think. Wrote to Mr. Lucas at Ben Rhydding informing him of the proceedings at the Committee on Tuesday last.

FRIDAY 5TH OF MAY 1848 – Read a few pages of a Preliminary Discourse to Milton's Prose Works by J. S. St. John. Took a short walk in the fields in the neighbourhood of Moss Lane. It has been a refulgent day. Everything seems to be refreshed and to rejoice in the coming of the eventide. O gentle nature! How full of medicinal and beautiful lessons thou art to weary human hearts.

SATURDAY 6TH OF MAY 1848 – Domestic unhappiness . This heavy living misery. A fit of distressing madness, tearing hair, and dashing head against the wall ?

SUNDAY 7TH MAY Delightful strolls in and about Moss Lane. Cleared out and arranged a box full of miscellaneous papers. – Languid in mind and body. Went to bed earlier than and as heavy hearted as ever. –

MONDAY 8TH MAY 1848 – Crawled down to town later than usual this morning. – wrote two letters – Canvassed for signatures to the Petition in Spring Gardens and the neighbourhood ...

[101] *More melancholy and resolve fills this page.*

[102] **TUESDAY 9TH OF MAY 1848.** Received a little insolent, mean-spirited epistle from that most irreverend 'Reverend' Wm. Smith of Rochdale in answer to my request that he would excuse me the remittance of five shillings last week.

Committee meeting. Wrote a scrap of rhyme. Something radically wrong with me both body and soul that makes me a constant mourner ...

More introspection follows, including the opening of the entry for Wednesday 10th of May 1848 then

Wrote to Mr. Lucas of Ben Rhydding. – Read Rousseau's short Essays on 'Amusements' 'History' and 'Education'. – Took a stroll up Moss Lane in the moonlight. The evening air rich with the sweets of Spring. Thinking bitterly about many things, among the rest that dirty little note from the pulpit charlatan at Rochdale galls me not a little. With what a ridiculously pompous air [103] he cants about 'punctuality' and 'extraordinary patience'. The hypocritical thief!

THURSDAY 11TH MAY 1848. Received a letter from Mr. Lucas at Ben Rhydding. At his request I wrote to Sharman Crawford M.P. respecting the presentation of the Petition of the Association in Rochdale.

The entry for Friday 12th May is yet again self-recrimination.

SATURDAY MAY 13TH. 1848. – What a sweet morning it is! The natural beauty and gladness of this rosy May tide will not be outdone either by the heart chilling habits of human life, or by deadening weight of human sorrows. It quite overpowers even this great, noisy, artificial city of Manchester with its heart warming loveliness. The air is full of sunshine, and the songs of birds and the scents of flowers. It is Saturday too, the flower morning! The market gardeners and flower growers who have mostly been up all night tying-up and sorting their bunches of flowers and herbs for this morning's market have come into town hours ago from the villages in a circle of some miles round the town, covered with dust to the eyelids, and with their brown, hearty [104] country looking hands and faces, fine living examples of the affects of simple living and healthy exercise. Let me lean a while at the corner of the street and see how gentle nature lights up the world of human eyes and bids all hearts be innocent and rejoice in the joys of Spring and woos them to throw aside their low feelings and despondencies and put their trust in the God who apparels the season in such inimitable sweetness and beauty. See how nature plays upon the human heart like a great master who knows the strings and can make them speak to his liking. O wonderful nature! Spirit of law and love! O great spirit that hath framed the world and they that dwell therein with such infinite power and love! How all things rightly considered, lead [?] us into the inexhaustible mystery of thy divine majesty! But a truce to such thinking [?].

See, here comes a fine young woman, with a springy step that tells everyone that watches her that the joy of this rosy May thrills through her, even to the tip of her light, delighted toes. God bless this happy and unsophisticated flower-lover! And keep her heart for ever as fair and pure and happy as nature herself who looks upon this beautiful specimen of her handiwork this sunny morning with delight that – she reminds me of Burns's lines.

[105]   Auld Nature swears the lovely dears
         Her dearest work she classes O
         The prentice-hand she tried a man
         And then she made the lasses O[4]

She has a 'posie' in her hand, made up of small flowers, tulips, red and white daisies, a tuft of delicate silver lilies, some violets and a tall spring of something green that swaggers above all the rest with a graceful plumy, nodding action. There is 'rosemary' and 'thyme', and 'lads love' too among that bunch of the sweets of Spring! I can smell them as she walks past me! O most delicious and friendly[?] odours! O dear native perfumes! How much I prize you above all the quack 'essences' that infect the air of Flirtland and Dandy-dom! How strongly they remind me of the old carved and lavender perfumed clothes-chest and of the odourous [sic] sweetness and purity of my white shirts given out by my careful mother from that sacred treasury! How it brings to mind my old grandmother's garden, by the brookside up in that quiet village among the moorland vales of Lancashire! My heart and

---

[4] Robert Burns's final verse of 'Green Grow the Rashes O', slightly misquoted.

thoughts are full of the green fields, and the wild flowers and sweet village hymns which I was taught to sing to quaint old sacred tunes, and all my childhood's sinless, careless happiness. The simple pious hymns of those saintly[?] days, and one especially is as powerful upon my heart as the rod of Moses is upon the rock. I never think of them, and of my poor old mother who taught them to me, that my heart is overpowered with [106] a melancholy delight – more absorbing for the time than any other feelings that awaken in my heart. – All this passed in my mind in a hundredth part of the time that it takes to write it, and my eyes followed the flower girl again as she tript away with her flowers scattering a stream of sweet odours as she went that made the little children run in the wake of her sniffing up the rich air as they ran, and crying out 'O's nice!' And her, and the flowers and the children, and all together were certainly delightful to every eye. See how tenderly the maiden grips her penny Eden and smiles timidly upon it, and seems as if she only needed an Adam to match the flowers and her, and earth would have done its utmost to make her happy. Her female acquaintances come to the doors, and call out after her, 'Oh, Mary, do let's smell!' 'Wherever did you get this?' 'At the green-grocers at the street end and you must be quick, they're going fast' – Away they run for 'Posies like Mary Nelson's' – And Mary goes on her way with her handful of flowers, drawing the sunshine, and cherishing the beauty of the day with the beautiful affection and simplicity that shines in all her motions. And lights up her eyes, and all the lineaments of her [107] sweet face. – Up comes a good-natured old gentleman with another bunch of May-flowers in his hand, and ever and anon he looks at them affectionately and buries his face, with the laugh that plays around his pleasant mouth – he buries it all in that rosy bush of the treasures of Spring. He wriggles his face in it half a minute, then, shutting his eyes, the gathering all his energies into one determined sniff at the flowers, tried to forget the world he had been living in, and revel an instant in the ecstasies of an Elysian fancy – But it is too much. Fancy could not outdo reality just then. He unburied his face again, and, with three or four drops of clear water winking beautifully about his nose and eyelids cried out 'Ah! That's fine!' then shades his face with his hands, and tried to look at the sun, and thought to himself, 'Well, this is a glorious world, after all!' Those little children ran after him crying out 'Give me a flower will you?'

[108] **SUNDAY 14TH MAY 1848** – Another sweet sunny May-day! Oh, how carelessly it has passed away! I am unhappy about the manner in which my Sabbaths are employed. Took a long walk with my wife. Wrote an hour at night while she read to me part of a religious tract.

MONDAY 15TH MAY – Wrote a letter for insertion in Shaw's circular.

There follows the beginning of a poem and then half a page is left blank. In fact there is almost a three month gap in the entries at this point.

[109] **THURSDAY 3RD OF AUGUST 1848.** Determined to give my heart to study and the acquisition of knowledge. – Read a page of Pope's 'Homer'.

FRIDAY 5TH OF AUG. 1848. – I feel as if I was girding up myself for a close and continuous course of study and my heart feels delighted in the anticipation of it. Bought a new copy of my old and true friend 'Thomas a Kempis' – A noble old monk! – A monarch! – I grieve when nobody thinks that such a feeling is near my heart, at the wild brood of follies that harbour in me, and that my life is fleeting away to so little account. I have less hope than I had of being such a man as I always wished in my heart to be, because my heart is harder and more worn into worldliness than when I was a child.

TUESDAY, 8 AUGUST 1848. – Read part of Combe's 'Remarks on National Education. – Prophetic presentiments respecting the termination of my year with the Association. Resolution to devote my life to the cultivation of the capacities which God has given me. Row in the street where we live. Brawling, disgusting women!

MONDAY, 9TH AUGUST 1848. – Among other things I have resolved to improve my hand-writing to which end I have been advised to write much larger than common. This is not allowable [110] in the Office Books, but I can figure as largely as I like in my own.

Waugh's handwriting does indeed grow larger and clearer at this point, having deteriorated after his earlier resolution to improve it. After a line gap he continues:

I have been disturbed with matrimonial sorrows all this day, and my mind filled with the most gloomy contemplations and questions respecting the intention and duration of this unhappiness. All that I do 'sicklied o'er with the pale cast of thought.'

Wrote some wretched rhyme, sighed over my indolence, and – went to bed. I could not sleep for some time for thinking about money I owe. O debt! Hell upon earth!

THURSDAY 7TH SEPTEMBER 1848 – Received another insolent epistle from the mean spirited whelp of a parson, who vows 'by all that he holds sacred' that if I do not pay him the sixteen shillings which is the balance of his account for instructing me in Latin, by tomorrow, he will put me in the Court. I wrote, telling him to send me no more hints and threats, but go about it, if he couldn't wait till I had money to rid me of debt and his insolent bluster.

[111] Sold more, nay almost the last of my books to meet contingencies. Nearly stript of external possession. My brains are fagged and weary with brooding over my own unhappy cares. I will rack the poor tired fools no more tonight, except with a page or two of 'Guy Mannering'.

FRIDAY, 8TH SEPTEMBER 1848 Rose a little earlier this morning. Breathe a little freer since I have written to Smith, the Unitarian parson. Looking out for a legal process! 'O my prophetic soul!' The law and the prophets.

SATURDAY, 9TH SEPTEMBER, 1848. – Here I sit on the bedside, my pen has been pending pensively [*'passively' replaced by pensively*] over my paper, that it might chronicle the first ghost of murdered thought that stalked through the sepulchral gloom of my chaotic mind ...

[112] *Waugh goes on through this page to inveigh against debt. 'It is akin to the devil!'*

[113] Hurrying to and fro all day to get in money for the Association. The result dispirited me.

More self-pitying reflections follow and also fill much of page 114.

SUNDAY 10 SEPTEMBER, 1848. – In the house the whole day. – Reading 'Guy Mannering.' – I have no clothes to go to church in and this is almost the only book I have left in the house just now, and I hardly think it would be here [115] but because the sale of it would have produced nothing, because it is the 'People's Edition' in loose soiled numbers. – Besides, I am happy to meet with anything which will give my thoughts a brief reprieve from the misery of a discordant house and vulgar brawls. Wrote part of a letter to the 'Examiner' on the Educational Plan. The day has been drizzly and dull, but the night came on beautifully clear and moonlight [*sic*], and I was delighted with it. I kept laying down my pen and going to the door and round the houses to bask in the silver light of 'MacFarlane's brat'.

MONDAY 11TH SEPTEMBER, 1848 Canvassing all day. Heard of Cameron's tuition of Jacob Bright in the Classics. – The news made me envious and emulous. – Another clear and beautifully calm moonlight night.

[116] *The entry for Tuesday, 12th of September, 1848 is taken up with more introspective reflection after attending a Committee meeting and this continues onto page 117.*

WEDNESDAY, 13TH OF SEPTEMBER, 1848 – Canvassing for Subscriptions. A dispiriting and unproductive job these moniless, meatless times. – I am a poor fist at this work too. – When I meet with men who either have not money to spare, or have not the disposition to spare it, – and these two comprise almost the whole number just now, – I have not that beggarly eloquence which can humbug them into a false generosity. – Therefore I get very little in my canvasses. – I hate to talk with a niggard about money, and there is so much sectarian prejudice against anything universal though ever so good that it is almost a wonder that men can agree to breathe the same unconventional air. Nature laughs at the pettifogging squabbles of these fools. The 'Plan' has yet to make itself widely known, too, and such work – public and private delving in the soil, – [118] such sowing of seed and harrowing, and watering, and patient waiting, before the hoped-for harvest can be won. – I have seen more of the pettiness, the disgusting meanness of sectarianism since I begun to canvass for this beautiful scheme of Public Education than ever I saw before in my whole life.

THURSDAY, 14 SEPTEM 1848. – Canvassing again. – My mind so unsettled that I do not go about my purposes with good heart. – Spent an hour in Wheatherley's Book Shop. Scribblers [*this word deleted*] and Parsons, and Wranglers, and Bookworms meet there. –Slater and theology. Proposed letters on the inspiration of the Bible.

FRIDAY, 15 SEPTR. 1848. – I have a passage of to-day's life to write down that is difficult to write, because the thought of it still distracts me. But I will not let it pass away unchronicled. I am nothing unless I unbosom myself, and then I am worse than nothing. [*A long line follows then*] ...

[119] I sat in the office this evening waiting by appointment for the coming of Mr. Samuel Lucas, the Chairman. I had an unpleasant foreboding of the intention of the visit. – I am conscious of manifold imperfections, and I felt justly apprehensive of dissatisfaction on that account. I felt disturbed by a tumult of after thoughts and regrets. How often has it been so with me before. I look back and there is one unbroken trail of incapacity and error behind me as far as the eye of memory can penetrate –––. I waited anxiously to know the upshot of what has been to me a year of unparalled [*sic*] discomfort and care and wretched struggling with the world within me and with a host of difficulties engendered by indiscretion. – Debt, domestic misery, and a half-spirited effort to fulfil [*sic*] the duties of an Office for which I am unfitted by previous habits and training. – Mr. Lucas came at last, and the uncommon courtesy of his manner increased my apprehension. After some preliminary politeness, he asked me to go with him to the inner room. 'Now then' I thought. He walked in, [120] and I followed and shut the door. 'I want to have a little talk with you about your prospects and the prospects of the Association' said he. 'Mr. Forrest would tell you what poor success Mr. McCall and I met with in Liverpool. Our endeavors [*sic*] to get money failed in every case but one, that of William Brown, M.P. who gave us £10. We found the time exceedingly unpropitious [*'to raising money' inserted*] and agreed respecting the absolute necessity of putting a stop to expenses, and we thought it advisable to close the offices, except on particular occasions, and carry on the agitation through the medium of the public journals in the most inexpensive manner possible. And the Committee who all have the kindliest feeling towards you, and are very desirous to save you any inconvenience, thought it most advisable for you to be on the lookout for some other employment and therefore commission me to give you a month's notice that you may have an opportunity of availing yourself of any chance of other employment that may offer in the meantime. We do not say that if you do not succeed by [121] the expiration of that time, we will not employ you longer, but money cannot be raised

for the purposes of this Association in the degree in which it was anticipated. I and the committee are resolved to limit their expenditure to their limited income. Do you think you could raise as much money by canvassing as would cover the current expenses of the Association? – I told him what an unparalled [*sic*] dearth of money I had found in my Canvasses up to this time. Nobody seemed to have enough for their necessary purposes and that besides, though I was willing to do all I could in the way of soliciting for subscriptions to the Association, I was one of the worst beggars in the world. I felt so conscious of the poverty of my powers that with an almost marked anxiety I asked him to tell me without reserve whether it was really this consideration of economy or my own incapacity that prompted the change desired by the Committee, and so kindly intimated to me. [122] He assured me it was purely a consideration of expence [*sic*], and that I have done the business of the Association to the perfect satisfaction of the Committee. I did not believe that for I felt that I had neither done the business to their satisfaction nor my own. 'They could not have had anybody with the varied qualifications required who could have [more?] fulfilled the duties of that office for the same remuneration that I had done.' – I felt that to be partly true, but I felt also that I was miserably deficient in the essential requisites of order, punctuality and perseverance. I am distrest with the consciousness of this. What shall I do? ... [*More self examination and resolution to do better then follows*] ... [123] After a few remarks respecting my chances of other employment, Mr. Lucas took his leave, assuring me of his desire to serve me in every way in his power. – I locked up the office and went houseward musing sadly.

Anxiety kept me turning from side to side sleeplessly all night.

SATURDAY, 16TH SEPTR, 1848. – I went into Weatherley, the Old Booksellers Shop at the top of the exchange Arcade, yesterday about noon and I found a scene of unhappy confusion. The old man in a great rage striking at his daughter Mary, while she screamed and voicferated [*sic*] with passionate stubbornness. – A quorum of the old man's fuddling chums had come in to exchange their cracks with him over a jorum of Finlater & Mackie's bottled porter. Mary was requested to fetch in the tipple. – The indignity protested against being made into a alehouse caidee for every drunken spunge [*sic*] that chose [124] to suck up swill in the shop, and vented some virulent abuse upon the slushy trio. She had propriety in her argument, but her language was certainly as intemperate as the occasion, and threw the old man into a violent passion, and, if I had not stept in between them, and endeavored [*sic*] to pacify them ['*he would have beaten her sorely[?]*' *inserted*]. He foamed, and she fainted, and the Bacchanalians fled and were no more seen. He curst and swore and trembled with passion a while, then followed them to mingle his superabundant steam [*deletions*] with the offices of the alehouse. I staid not long for her tongue began to unload a cargo of treasured epithets which she pelted after the discomfited drinkers without mercy. – I went away thinking melancholically of the misery of such scenes as those I had just witnessed. –

The number of emendations in describing this scene suggest that, as with the 'Mayday' scene earlier, Waugh is deliberately writing a piece of 'literary description' here rather than just jotting down what he saw.

Canvassed part of the day. – Got subscriptions amounting to £2.10 I am ['*oppressed with a sense of pettiness in all I do*' *inserted*]. Read scraps in Family Herald and the 1st page of Emerson's Essay on 'Nature'. I purpose to paraphrase those passages in his works which seem to me to contain most [125] originality and beauty or force of thought or of expression.

Waugh then commits himself to new resolutions including:

Early Rising
Three hours walking, fencing, boxing, wrestling, and other manual exercises
Daily cold washing and friction
Fit food in kind and quantity
Sufficient clothing
Proper recreation

[126] ... I am almost bookless now, but I begin to think that will be more good than evil to me. I shall pay the closer attention to what I have. My whole library, with the exception of half a dozen choice works is squandered. But what then? I have the Bible and Shakespeare, and George Herbert and Thomas a Kempis – and Bunyan each of which is a library of thought in itself. And I have now a much extended knowledge to guide my choice in the famed gems of the world's literature, when I want them, and have the chance of procuring them ... [*More moralizing follows.*]

SUNDAY, 17 SEPTEMBER 1848. – Staid at home the whole day, because I have no clothes fit to go out in. – Reading and writing the greater part of the day. Resolved to write down the resolutions of the following day, and review them the following day.

[127] Resolved

That I will make a list of my debts.

That I will write to Cousin Grace.

That I will revise my letter to the Examiner tomorrow.

A very feeble poem completes the page.

[128] **MONDAY 18 SEPTEM. 1848** – Rose a little earlier this morning. The air beautifully clear and bracing. I will do a little arithmetic today. I called upon Macdougall the Arithmetician last week and enquired what his terms of teaching were. He told that he charged One Pound for teaching the shortest methods of Arithmetical calculation, and that any time of the day which was convenient to me would be convenient to him. I made no arrangement with him, as I had no money, but I have a great want of that discipline which would train my mind to method and precision. I canvassed in Faulkner Street this forenoon, with no effect in the respect of money-getting ...

In the after part of the day, I canvassed for subscriptions in Faulkner Street again, without success, however, except one little solitary shilling. – I went into a foreign house (Ree's). I entered into conversation with the cashier respecting the Plan of Public Education devised by the 'Lancashire Public School Association'. He approved the scheme highly, so far as he knew it, but I found that he was not thoroughly acquainted with the nature of it. Had a vaccillating [*sic*] desire for the inculcation [129] of doctrinal religion in all schools, private or public. Of course I contended for the injudiciousness of admitting sectarian doctrines prematurely into Schools for the young, and the impractibility of establishing any really National System of Education efficient for the wants of the whole people in this respect if such elements were admitted into schools intended for the public benefit. His notion wavered respecting this. He was, however, a liberal and a pious man in his disposition – although a Wesleyan Methodist, – a body of religionists which, as a whole, have wandered so far from the simple purity of their famous founder that they are become proverbial for their pharisaic pride and intolerance. The discussion of this question of Public Education led us into spiritual enquiries. He began to dispute rather loosely about the foreknowledge of God, fate, free will, original sin, the doctrine of the Atonement, and the character of Scriptural revelation. That certainly is a formidable list of subjects. Of course we settled it all. However, as these subjects passed in review in the course of the conversation, I pointed my finger at them, sometimes with a skeptical [sic] allusion for the purpose of bringing out the explanatory remarks of my Methodistical disputant, and an intelligent and devout young foreigner who joined with his friend in defence of their common orthodoxy. They had both so much liberality, intelligence and courtesy mingled with their peculiar opinions that I conversed with them with pleasure and benefit till time and business separated us in the dusk of the evening.

[130] I will, for many reasons make this book my diary, and my exercise book. I have no Arithmetic in my possession, but for exercise.

A complicated sum takes up some quarter of the page.

No more of that to-night. I'll go to bed, after I have written my letter, and revised the one to the Examiner. My book, like my life is sullied as I go on.

Resolved

To write to Joseph Butterworth tomorrow night.

TUESDAY 19 SEPT 1848. – As I canvassed for subscriptions today in Deansgate, among others, I entered the shop of a Shoe Dealer. As I stood explaining the nature of the Educational Plan of the Association to the proprietor of the shop, who seemed a snappish and illiberal man, a poor woman came in in a tattered dress, and begged, with a timid and peculiarly painful expression of countenance, that bespoke the genuineness of her poverty, for a halfpenny or a handful of meal, for [131] her children and herself were starving. He instantly bade her in a blustering tone 'be off, he had nothing for her nor her children.' The woman burst into tears and walked away. I would dearly have liked to knock the fellow down for his damned unfeeling insolence. But there was a redeeming angel near. There was a woman in the shop busy among the shoes – whether she was wife or daughter I know not. – but I know that she had a graceful figure, and a handsome and intelligent face. She put down the shoes out of her hands, and as the starving creature walked away, her face assumed an indescribable expression of heartfelt sympathy, and she said very lowly, as she looked after her through the windows, 'Poor woman, that's a heart-breaking sight.' She then stept briskly from behind the counter, and walked after her. I followed and saw her overtake the unhappy body and addressing her very kindly, she gave her money. The woman thanked her with earnest feeling. I watched the angel of mercy as she walked away. Deansgate never seemed so grand to me before. God bless her gentlewoman's heart! I shall never forget her.

[132] *Presumably the diary records separate days at this point but, for the rest of the week Waugh does not indicate this.*

I rambled so far in the moonlight last night that I had no disposition for writing much. It is now early in the morning. I must be off.

I have been busy copying and disputating the Honorary Secretary's Circular of Invitation to the Soiree at the Committee rooms on the 28th instant. My weak brain has been so overwhelmed with distracting emotions this last year that mistakes have frequently crept into my daily business. This has been remarked in me by several members of the Committee, and I am in a fair way for establishing the reputation of a habitual blunderer. I am resolved to master this bad habit. I will endeavour to train my mind to strength, calmness and precision. – I have had no time for canvassing today. Schemes of living flitting fitfully through my mind, as almost everything does, but nothing stable. My wife and Sally are talking at such a rate just now that I cannot think as I write.

I went into Wheatherley's Shop today, and met with William Audrey. Audrey begun to give an account of his peregrinations through a great deal of England, Ireland and Scotland, selling books by hand. The recital of his adventures pleased me. He gave so many evidences of brave self-reliant effort under difficulties.

[133] *More than half of this page is taken up with an arithmetical calculation.*

I started from Manchester at two o clock and came up home into Hulme two miles at least. I was very hungry, and had neither money nor meat in the house, and now I am here there is hardly potatoes enow for a meal, and I am so hampered and harried for money that I see no way of raising the next meal but by disposing of four old Books that I have.

It must be done. I shall be bookless again, But I can always borrow a good volume to read, and then I have the dear Old Booksellers shops and stalls and windows and – oh, inexhaustible, inexpressible pleasure – the sublime volume of Nature, the Book of God – a new edition every moment.

[134] I have canvassed again this afternoon, and after many fruitless calls and salutations and explanations and peregrinations among tradesmen and merchants of all nations, I expended the expiring energies of the day in actually humbugging two printers out of a pair of half crowns, which I bore away with a relieved mind, altho' the only trophies of the day's begging expedition. I make miserable progress in begging. But the complaints of the depression of trade and the overpowering burthening of the poor rates is above all parallel. Everybody's expenses exceeding their income. The rich curtailing expenses, sick of the outgo without return. The ear of benevolence deaf with repeated calls. Tradesmen selling their stocks in every direction to meet demands. The workhouses full. Printers busy printing 'to let' and 'to be sold by auction'. Every morning revealing numerous 'moonlight flits' of the last night. The poor giving up their houses, and clustering together for economy in the cheapest possible dwellings [?]. Those who have employment trembling with fear and subscribing their shillings to Emigration clubs, and those who have no work – begging and starving.

More self reflection follows.

[135] My clerical torturer has not troubled me since I gave him that last 'welt o'th mouth'.

The rest of the page is taken up with a calculation and the verse of a poem.

[136] **SATURDAY 23 SEP 1848** – I am anxious to 'reform in words' some passages of yesterday's life, but haven't time just now. I must be off.

I stept into J. Race Horner, the solicitor's Office yesterday to ask him for a subscription to the Public Schools Association. He is a Wakefield acquaintance of mine.[5] I sat down with him a while and talked over the bygone time, and the current of changes that has come

---

[5] Waugh had worked for two years on the Wakefield Journal before returning to live in Rochdale. (Robertson, 1881 p. 170)

over us from then to now. We made an exchange of reminiscences and revelations and confessions, and reviewed the characters and fortunes of some of our acquaintances. Our much respected Tom Lamb was steadily prosperous. Banks was just about to make a triumphant exit from the bondage of his Articles of Clerkship, and was full of high hopes. Slack – (by the way, my acquaintance with him is very rusty, and I never had much liking for one who I judged of heaven only knows whether justly or not – as clever little buffoon, – whose talents had no real wisdom to steer them – but heaven make us charitable to one another under all circumstances, what man judge another?) Slack is married to a lady with some property, which with his practice brings him £700 a year. [*Name deleted 'had broken through all restraints and responsibilities and was living dissolutely and' inserted*] was gone to spend a fortnight in Germany with his dearly-beloved puppy of a friend – S – the Professor of English at Dresden College. – They are whelps of one litter, those two clever literary fools – [137] Horner himself was going to marry in a week from that day. He could not rest by day, nor sleep by night for the anxious thoughts of this important contract. It made him ill. He gave me a ludicrous account of the difficulties and mischances of his bachelorship while living in Manchester. He was determined to marry, and felt confident it was for the best. Chance had thrown him in the way of a young lady who, though she had no money, had every other other [*sic*] enrichment that can dower an angel of the earth. His friends objected to the match because of her pennilessness, and pressed upon him to look out for 'somebody' that had 'something'. We joined in one fervent chorus and damned his friends – and he swore he would marry her next week. My own story was strangest of all. The course of events that had befallen me since last we met were [*sic*] singular. The string of mischances, – extreme triumphs and discomfitures made up a short narrative that sounded very wild even as far as I ventured to tell it, and I did not tell the whole, partly because he would not have believed it, and partly because he was not exactly the man I should have told it to freely, and with an easy and confident mind. However, I opened to him a passage or two of the Book, – as much as I thought he could interpret, and perhaps more, but I kept the remainder closed. The most interesting part of my life for some years past [138] has been the period of my courtship and marriage – the wild, disturbed current of the one, and the difficulties and unhappinesses that have begirt the other, and my consolation and support must be in the effort to live virtuously, to observe, to know and to feel the glory of God and the nature of nature – and to reveal beautifully all my thoughts and feelings again in language ... [*More philosophizing fills the rest of the page.*]

[139] I canvassed for subscriptions till night, and with small success and satisfaction. At night I lockt up the Office, and altho' – while I have admired Wheatherley the Old Bookseller for the unprejudiced tone of his mind, the strength of his nature, and the independence of his spirit, I have been so often disgusted by the coarseness of his habits and language that I have vowed internally that I would enter there no more – so strong has the habit grown upon me, and so great is the enticement of <u>hearty speech</u> with me, – and so weak is my resolution to resist the enticement of bold and beautiful expression even though it reveal and perhaps strengthen improprieties of thought that I detest both in myself and in others, I went into the dear old Book Shop once more. The books themselves are an inexpressible, an almost unconscious attraction to me. I leave my mistakes and annoyances, and the whole whirlwind of life's pestilences and sorrows, at the door where these are, and I sit down for a while, sheltered, relieved, and strengthened among these fine old silent speakers, that smile, approve and cheer, and frown, reprove and admonish with such serene and solemn friendliness. I went into the Shop again and, after saluting with my heart and eye certain noble reliques of the world-famed priests of virtue and nature and the soul, the locality of which remains [140] I knew on the surrounding shelves, where they stood with a kind of beseeching look beset with a multitude of drossy babblers, a vast majority of more verbal garbage and froth waiting patiently till some heaven – commissioned congenial spirit fostered them restored them to the fulfillment of their high offices. After glancing round and greeting these with lowly internal reverence, I fell into conversation again with my bibliophilopic friend. He proposed a walk to his son Roger's newly-opened Bookshop in Withy Grove, to see how it lookt now that he had got gas fit into it. He gave me part of about 20 vols. of rubbishy books to carry, which he was going to sell Roger for eighteen pence. They were poor stuff, complete trash in the book market at least, Methodist Magazines and such like palaver. He could not sell them in his shop or at his stall in Shudehill, where

so many of those who purchased were guided in their choice by the mere outward appearance and bulk and big assemblage of the book – They would ask the price of a lump of printed paper with backs on and then weigh it in their hands, and look at the number of pages and say 'Whare Sam O'Robins bought one wi' moor pages in it nur this, for th'hauve o'that brass.' Of course there is a class of customers who walk the round of the stalls in every part of the town, [141] whose educated eyes continually peer through the files of rubbish for the gems of literature. Mechanical booklovers and book hoarders, and dodgers in the book-trade to each of whose five senses it is a perfect feast to root and dabble in stores of old Books. These all swarm and gloat over piles of old Books like ravens over a dead body – some to satisfy one species of hunger, some another. And sometimes gaunt intelligent faces sometimes flit round them looking for their friends and when they find one, ask his price with eager anxious looks, and, if they have the money, dab it down hastily and flee away with their treasure to some monastic corner. And poor scholars and students of all classes and conditions of life haunt these old Book Stalls and Shops. I have sometimes thought that knaves and fools oftener jostle the salt of the earth there than anywhere else in cities and towns. But here in Shudehill, one of the oldest and dirtiest and lowest purlieus of the town, where the literary trash of Manchester is chiefly congregated and vended on a host of stalls when it is at all fine weather, and in little dirty dark shops and cellar-holes when it is foul – here the illiterate customers and cheap lump hunters almost invariably come to make their bargains. As we went along Whetherley [sic] told me what trouble his son Roger had been to him – how shiftless and inattentive to business he had been for many years. He had been a continual burden to him. He had helpt him while he would not help [142] himself and couldn't do because he did not know how. But at last to say it was no use he was always 'ofter his bones' and he was a 'damned scamp' beside, so he 'turned Turk' and wouldn't help him any longer 'not a blasted hawpoth'. Since then he said Roger had struggled for himself with his stall, and had gained confidence in himself, and lived carefully and now he had opened the little Shop ['we were going to' inserted] and was getting on like a house on fire.

We went into Roger's Shop – a little dirty-looking nook about two yards square, the floor broken in some places and the holes 'repaired' with pieces of old worm eaten plank and orange boxes. One piece of the wall was tolerably fitted up with cobbled shelves, made out of rough boards, and filled with the choice of his stock, among which were a few good books – one corner had about three mounds of unsorted rubbish piled up slantingly one upon another, another lot upon an old rickety table, and in the middle of the floor a pyramid of literary muck thrown down like a load of rocks. Everything was dirt and confusion. Roger sat at the board under the windows in his shirt sleeves, and with his face smuttied o'er, labelling and patching up old Books. He had no gas yet, and the place was lighted up by two thick candles, which 'swaled' and flickered and slavered their fat with the wind that puffed at them through a pair of holes in the window. [143] One of the candles was in a rusty iron stick, and the other was ungrafted into the heart of a large potatoe [sic] of the 'Bloody Roger' clan. And the flame at the top of the candles wriggled and twisted and swaggered and lost its head as if highly indignant at the idea of his grease associating with the lowborn lumper into whose society he had been so unceremoniously thrust. – 'Uncle Jem' made a chair of old Books, and I squatted down upon an inverted clothes basket. Roger paid his father eighteen pence for the Books, and went out at his request for a bottle of porter, which was handed round in a tay-cup. He ['Roger' inserted] had a pair of massive ornamented old iron spurs of the kind worn by the Puritan soldiery in Cromwell's time. They were very heavy and large, and the rowels above an inch long. He asked a sovereign for them. – We came away after a while, and the old man called to tell his daughter to lock up his shop and take charge of the key, and then I walked with him homeward up Deansgate. As he passed one of his houses of call, he proposed going in to drink a bottle of porter. Feeling a strong dislike to such places, and being squeamish about the stomach, I objected. He pressed, and I agreed, after buying something to eat, that I would come in after him. I bought half a pound of Pork pie, and following him in eat [sic] it to the Porter. He would have stopt on drinking, but I was ill at ease [144] in mind and body, and anxious to go. We came out and went on till I came to a cook's Shop where I bought a pennorth of 'Yorkshire Pudding' and I eat [sic] it as I went on further till I came to a little cellar where an old Barber stands on the steps every night screaming out 'Ros-'tatur-at-ot' while his old wife hobbles about superintending the roasting of thumping 'Pink Eyes' and 'Red Farmers' and brewing 'prime Nettle Beer' to swill the lusty esculent down the throats of her singular variety of castaways. – I often stop there to burn my mouth with her fine hot potatoes, and cool it again with Nettle Beer at halfpenny a bottle, and to have a little talk with the bald-headed barber and his wife, and the folks that come into the shop. He saluted me as I passed, and I ran in for a 'Penorth' and put them in my pocket, and eat [sic] them as we went on. – When we came to the end of Bridgewater Viaduct, he insisted on our having a parting glass at the 'Blue Bell'. I didn't like to go in, for I had neither inclination for drink nor money to spend on it. He pressed, and I, always ready to contemplate humanity under a new plane followed him into the vault. He ordered two glasses of rum and water, and we sat down. He groped for his snuff box. He had left it at the shop. I wanted a pinch too, and we scanned the faces in the place to see if [145] we could read 'Snuff-taker' in any. They were all rough hardy-brown faced farm labourers with one exception. We looked in vain at them, but there sat in the corner a tall, thin old mechanic with a long and sallow face. There was hope there. Weatherley got up and asked him, and he lugged out his box in comment. We began to talk and he made some allusion to 'Burns' with whose works he was intimately acquainted, and could quote and repeat with astonishing correctness in every respect, and could appreciate with a feeling congenial to the spirit of the author. He spoke with water standing in his eyes of the humanity of spirit and the delicate and fervent love which pervaded the Works of Burns. He repeated some of the choicest examples with taste and feeling.

The course of his conversation evinced that he had read much and well. He was an intelligent, generous and humane man with a strong sense of justice even though – (oh, ye intemperate advocates of Abstinence) – even though he sat drinking here in a liquor vault among 'publicans and sinners.' His presence there, and for such a purpose, was perhaps no evidence of his intelligence, nor mine either – I know it might easily be assumed so. – but, however, let that pass. – I do not think of attempting to defend either him or myself on that score, because it is hardly worth the trouble, – but he was a noble fellow, and [146] I enjoyed his company. He had from necessity been kept to hard labor [sic] ever since he was able to do anything at all. But ever since he was a lad he lost no opportunity of 'grabbing a book' when he would either borrow one or scrape money enough to buy one. We sat and chatted till Eleven o'clock when we each took our way home through the rain.

The rest of the page is taken up with a calculation.

[147] **SUNDAY, 24TH SEPTEMBER 1848.** Incessant rain today. – Staid at home writing all day.

Further invocation to God follows.

MONDAY 25TH SEPTEMBER 1848 – I feel dull and sickly with a bad cold this morning. – Copying letters of invitation to the Soiree. – Canvassed for Subscriptions in Lower King Street. Had a bit of hearty conversation with Nathan Gough, the Engineer, respecting the Plan which he ardently admires. He heartily denounced the fine fallacies that oppose Secular education because unmixed with doctrinal teaching. Pure practical morality and intelligence the natural foundation of both physical and spiritual welfare, and not a blind acquiescence in theological opinions. – He was a healthy-looking, good-humoured, warm-hearted, intelligent, and courteous old man, and ever and anon kept tugging out his silver snuff box and [148] feasting his proboscis with right good will. He spoke bitterly against the parsons of the age as a tribe of unfaithful prayer spinners, the conservers of mental ignorance, the practical foes of religion, and the propagators of practical infidelity. He thought those ministers of religion who opposed the establishment of a National Plan of Secular Education in England, gave the most convincing proof of their ignorance of the nature of Man, and of the laws of God as revealed in man and in Nature. They seemed to delight to preach incomprehensible jargon to congregations that could only with difficulty comprehend the most understandable part of the <u>doctrines</u> of theology. – Intelligence seemed to be a dread; there was more of it already in the world than they could turn to <u>their</u> account, with all the preaching and praying power they could command and all their immense endowments and expenditures. – I left Mr. Gough and went on and called upon Cartledge, the Bookseller to see if I could induce him to subscribe. At first he objected to the levying of a rate for Public Education, but after some conversation and explanation respecting the just and economical character of such a rate, he subscribed. After I left Cartledge I entered a Tailors Shop (Thomas's) where I entered into conversation with the Master-Tailor – an intelligent young fellow, – and a young, illiberal, and domineering suckey of a [149] classical scholar, proud as a parrot of his ill-remembered Greek and Latin, which nobody would have known that he knew anything about if he had not taken some pains to inform us of the fact! He was, after all, a dull senseless chap, and to me didn't seem to have half the practical knowledge and intelligence that I have sometimes found among the better class of doffers in the factories. We wrangled a short time upon the subject of Public Education. He had the loosest, wildest notions upon the subject that ever I met with, or rather he had no notion at all upon the matter, – neither facts nor reasons, except a vague opinion that it was 'no use educating the people', they were 'better without it', unless they could receive a 'thorough education' –' a little learning was a dangerous thing', it 'only made them Chartists and infidels, and such like', – 'they were better as they were'. I asked him what he meant by 'a thorough education'. 'Why, a classical education', – he meant to say, 'such a one as I have had,' and truly, I thought if that produced no better effect upon them, than – so far as I could judge from his conversation – it had had upon the college-bred sample before me – it would 'indeed be useless except as a meaningless boast.' – However, I do not slight that which is in itself [*good seed' inserted*] because it happens to fall into bad soil, and produce nothing, or worse than nothing. The pearl is no less a pearl because it is hidden in an oyster, or hung in he nose of a pig, or the ear of a whore [*this word crossed out*].

[150]   'If honest nature made you fools
             What sairs your grammars
        Ye'd better taen up spades and shools,
            Or knapping hammers.'[6]

    I certainly think that the rough struggle of poverty and hard work would teach some of these conceited classical boobies more true knowledge than all their college parrot lore – and would be the only [*'educational' inserted*] touchstone that can turn [*'their book-learning'[?]* inserted] to golden wisdom.
    But,

---

[6] Part of a verse from Burns's 'Epistle to John Lapraik'

They think to climb Parnassus
By dint of Greek.

How blind they! The perpetual influence of human action in the discipline of life is too often left out of the great account of human training. The world is a college; life is a curriculum of study, man is the student, and God is the principal.

After leaving this gingerbread scholar, and – what I marked the more because of the contrast between them – the intelligent 'snip' who took the measure of his body while I took the measure of his brains, – that is so far as I could discover that he had any. – I went office-wards, thinking over the events of the day as I went.

TUESDAY 26TH SEPTEMBER, 1848 Discord on the hearthstone! O this unhappy, lovless [*sic*] fireside!

'I could write, but they would see't
Whistle o'er the lave o't'

I walked down to the town with an unhappy, heaving heart to carry with me, and I could not lay it down awhile and rest me; I was forced to carry it on.

[151] *The first half of the page is taken up with another calculation.*

WEDNESDAY, 27TH SEPTEMBER, 1848 – Wild miserable weather in my mind. Clouds and tempests. 'The heart knoweth its own sorrows.' It is night and I am weary. I felt delightfully refreshed today, as I always do from reading Burns. But even the pleasure I feel intensely in conversing with the noble soul of the King of Scottish Bards is tinged with saddened reflections.

Making preparations for the Soiree tomorrow at which a host of literary men of Manchester, Doctors Vaughan, Davidson, Beard, Mainzer and Hodgson, and two Members of Parliament are to be present.

[152] **THURSDAY 28 SEPTEMBER 1848.** I feel so blank this morning that I have nothing to write about just now. [*An underlining follows, then*]
Eleven o'clock
I have just come from the soiree of the Lancashire Public School Association, at which there has been a large attendance of the most

famed intelligent men in the county. They all seemed to me to be more remarkable for clear perceptions of what are called 'practical affairs' than for fine imagination. There was more of mere brain eye-sight that [*sic*] of the fine perceptions of a delicate and intelligent enthusiasm. – There were no men there who thought and felt and spoke in the attitude of Emerson and Cameron. But this project is a noble one, and has in itself the element of success, and its success in this country will be greatly accelerated by the fine phalanx of determined and practically intelligent men who have espoused it with a steadiness of purpose which in the upshot is not wont to dishonour the character of their judgement. – As I sat listening to their speeches – although I heard nothing very remarkable in them – I felt stirred by a strengthened impulse to improve my own faculties ...

More resolutions to improve follow into page 153, and melancholy as 'This damned debt disturbs me again. I have no peace (nor piece) for it'. This continues into the entry for Friday, 29th September 1848 which ends on page 154 with 'wrote to John Allan Slater as I rested in bed'. The entry for Saturday 1st October, 1848, also on page 154 continues a record of poor health.

[155] **SUNDAY, 2 OCTOBER, 1848.** Copied the Association's accounts. Re-wrote letter to Allan Slater. Went to Granby Row Catholic Chapel at Evening Service. Felt disgusted by the formal unfeeling manner in which the priest hurried through that part of the prayers in which occurs 'Jesus, the spouse of Virgins', 'Jesus, the Joy of Angels.' 'Tantum ergo Sacramentum.'

When the service ended I went with Mary Ann homeward. On the road we came to the little humble chapel of the 'Latter-day Saints', with its broken front, in Stretford Road. We went in. The inside was exceedingly clean, and simple, and unadorned by anything but its beautiful simplicity, and its chaste cleanliness. I sat and listened till the end of the Service, but I must confess that I could not from what I heard, gather the peculiarities of the doctrines of the sect that frequented there. No small compliment that [*a gap in the writing*]. Went to bed late again. The devil torments my ['*irresolute*' *inserted*] mind.

MONDAY 3ᴿᴰ OCTOBER Jars on the hearth again! No putting ones feet down for them. There is no home where there is no peace, no affinity x x x x x x x

Mary Ann off by the train to Rochdale, bag and baggage. Her box of clothes, the rocking chair I bought her, and other favourite oddments.

– I [156] followed her at night by the train, with a load of anxiety. When I reached the station I posted away to her Aunt's house, expecting to find her there. The door of the Lodge where she lived in the old green lane was locked and all dark within. I enquired at 'Th'Hease' and found that 'Sally' had gone to Milnrow in the fore part of the day, to see her cousins, John Clegg, the Grocer and his wife. I waited a while uneasily, then went down to 'Owd Jenny's' at 'Front Lodge', to seek for Sally and thence to Milnrow after her. The night was dark and wet and the road 'slutchy'. I reached there at half past ten. Sally had gone back by a different road, at the time I was coming. Blessed are they that expect disappointment, for they shall not be disappointed, thought I. However I sat and talked a while with John and Sally Clegg, who guessed by my downcast image I suppose that some new disturbance had broken out in the connubial department. He was very wary and chary of speech upon the subject, and seemed to think that married folk were best left to settle their disputes without interference from a third party And I think so too, unless some wise friend could hint to each privately their individual defects in such a manner as to induce them to put them to careful mending, and to bear and forbear ['with each other' is here crossed out] and help one another's infirmities, and not magnify them. – They invited me to sup with them on 'Cockles and Mussels', ale, oatcake and [157] beautiful butter, and cheese, and 'curren moufin'. – I left there at half past eleven and walked to Rochdale again through a heavy shower of rain. The remembrance of that night reminds me of Old Lear's unhappiness. At last I reached the Lodge – a walking lump of dishclout. I knockt, and Sally came to the door, half-drest, and shouted 'hello','hoo's theer'. 'It's me' said I, and she opened the door and let me in with an expression of countenance considerably affected by the first edition of the news of our fireside riot, which had reached her before me by an interested and prejudiced reporter. I found my wife sitting on the 'Couch cheer i'th'kitchen'. Small salutation passed between us for a few minutes. I doffed my wet things and put on old dry ones. We began gradually to talk, and to warm and embitter as we talked till at last we grew heated into passion by conversation x x x x x x.

At about two o'clock in the morning we went weary to an uncongenial bed. I rose in the morning in time for the nine o'clock train for Manchester, and departed from the town as miserable in mind as when I came to it the previous night. 'Quid dejicis te, anima tua?

Et quare conturbas mea? Spera in Deo, quoniam ad tua soufitebor illi: Salutare multus mea' – I canvassed for Subscriptions in Manchester the whole day, and when I got to the house called 'home' in Hulme at Eleven o'clock at night, I found Mary Ann and her [158] Aunt Sally had just arrived from Rochdale. They had walked the whole distance.

Waugh's troubles seem to make the date of entries to this page very unreliable.

WEDNESDAY, 4ᵀᴴ OCTOBER, 1848 – I am writing the minutes [*sic*] (?) of this and the following six days from a rather dim remembrance of what I thought and did at the time. I know I was employed part of the day writing letters respecting subscriptions and finished my day in Manchester with an hour's lounge in the Old Bookshop.

THURSDAY, 6ᵀᴴ OCTOBER, 1848. [*actually the 5th*] – I have just now no recollection of the transactions of the day, nor have I the disposition to wait for them springing up, nor to rack my brains with rooting for them just now. See how bleak and weak my mind is frequently!

FRIDAY 7ᵀᴴ OCTOBER, 1848 [*the 6th*] Running up and down Manchester all day for subscriptions. 'The times are out of joint'. Rich men are bemoaning the decrease of income, and indignant at the least trespass upon their accustomed luxuries, and poor men are looking with anxious hopeless hearts to the right and left for labour wherewith to procure the sustenance of bare life for the present hour, and are full of wretched forebodings for the future.

SATURDAY 9ᵀᴴ OCTOBER 1848. [*the 7th*] – Went to Rochdale at noon by the train to get Subscriptions. – Pitiful success. – I got £1 from Thomas Chadwick, and a few smaller Subscriptions. – Slept at the Lodge again. – Mary Ann had [159] come from Manchester by the Omnibus to Middleton, and thence to Rochdale on foot. I am so scant o' cash, and so keenly worried for the little I have that I tremble when I finger it sometimes.

SUNDAY, 8ᵀᴴ. OCTOBER, 1848. Stayed at the Lodge till the Evening. I had not clothing fit for Sunday appearances on the streets. At dusk I sallied forth in search of old congenial comrades. From one house to another I went through all the accustomed runs without success. Where could they be? The night was dark and wet. On my way home I called at my half-sister Ann's to see my Mother. I was fain to find her in better health and spirits than usual. I went on my way and bethought me, as it was in the road, that I would peep into Sam Stott's, the bastard Methodist Parson that keeps the 'Old Chapel House' Inn, to see if the ranting clan had gathered there. There they were sure enough, a whole room full. – There was a general whoop when I went in. I sat an hour with them disputing respecting the existence of God – which the whole of those present, except myself, professed to disbelieve. Wm. Mallalieu, an intelligent and hearty man, about forty-five years of age, owner of the Jacky Lane [?] Brow Woollen Mill, challenged me to a correspondence on the subject. – I accepted it, and agreed to write first. I walked with Mallalieu and James Daly to their end of the town. Daly left us, and I went on through [160] the fields to Jacky Brow. Supt with him on Bread and Cheese and Celery and came back at midnight through the rain [?]. I crept into my nest in the wood and slept soundly till morning.

MONDAY, 9TH OCTOBER, 1848. – I went by the nine o'clock train to Manchester. The country is a delight to me! It is more congenial to me a thousand times than the city! I have a constant yearning for it. – The oft returning images of the beautiful solitudes of nature make me both sigh and rejoice amidst the smoke and bustle, and foolish effrontery and cunning of town life. When I got to the office, Forrest's hypocritical eyes began to peer about for some pettifogging opportunity of fault finding. He began to talk in an inconsiderate strain as usual. – I suddenly rose in hot and hasty reply, and feeling that he was addicted to browbeating I believe he, as suddenly lowered his tone, and we parted for the day with a ludicrous effort to assume the usual free friendliness of manner. – I took the one o'clock train to Warrington, with the view of collecting Subscriptions from the friends of the Association in that town. I was delighted again with the appearance of the country as we passed along, and especially with the expanse and wild beauty of Chat Moss and the picturesque appearance of the country beyond the Moss towards Preston. The rain fell fast as I entered the fine old town of Warrington. How different it appeared to what it did when, in the early part of my apprenticeship, I ran away through it to Liverpool to become a sailor.[7] – I looked out for a [161] decent, old-fashioned little Alehouse.

---

[7]   Waugh did indeed 'run away to sea' as a boy, but soon turned back. (Milner 1893)

(I love Temperance, but I don't like Temperance Hotels) or a Barber's shop where I could be shaved, wash my face, comb my hair, brush my wet hat and coat, and shake my entire disordered and much splashed and spangled exterior into as comely an appearance as possible without the necessity of incurring expences [sic] which I could not bear. 'Tis true my expences [sic] were chargeable upon my employer, but I had resolved to have one good hearty meal after I had done my business in the town, and I felt no inclination for any smattering sups nor snacks before then. I popt into the first Barber's shop I met with, in Butter Market Street, and, the Barber being out, was shaved by his brother, a poor deformed fellow, who was so warped and ['stunted and' inserted] and shrunken in his figure that he could hardly lay hold of my nose when I was seated. He was so tremulous in the operation, and performed it so timidly and awkwardly that I winked and wizened, what with his dull razor, and a powerful consciousness of the bloody jeopardy that my jaw covers were in, and intensely prayed that this miserable chin-mower would fly away with his scythe, like old Time, even though he left half the job undone. – However, we got through it without mishap, and brushing my hat and my 'Brutus' and 'tittivating' my soiled habiliments a little, I sallied out to seek for 'Rylands and Sons,' Ironmonger. It was close by. – I found that Peter Rylands, the <u>man</u> of the family, was away on business in Ireland [162] and I knew, therefore that mine was a thriftless errand. I met his brother T. G. Rylands, – who seemed to me a bombastic sort of youth as noisy and as ready, and as empty as a hollow hammered barrel. He advised me to attempt nothing in the way of canvassing until his brother arrived back. That was reasonable enough as I knew that his brother Peter had had the whole of the agitation of the question in his own hands and by his personal efforts had obtained almost all the adhesions to this Association which it owns in Warrington and his personal assistance would be a considerable assistance to a stranger canvassing for Subscriptions, besides, being absent and unconsulted, he might look upon it as an unceremonious intrusion upon his own preserves. Altogether I thought it best to come away, and go again some other day. However I called on T. G. McMinnies, Peter Ryland's friend. He looked a hopeless look, complained of the hardness of the times, advised me to attempt no further till Peter came back. As much

See also entry for 4/5/50.

fuss about this 'Peter' as if he was the famous Peter of heaven ['*thought I*' *inserted*].

McMinnies fumbled a while musingly in his pocket, pickt his teeth, he had just had his dinner, – looked through the window sulkily, and at last tugged out half a sovereign with a most uncharitable and compelled air, and threw it down as if he was throwing a turd at a dog. If it had been for me I would have thrown it at him again, – but it was not, – so I pocketed all together, gave him a receipt for the money, and walked away. – – I called to see the Rev Philip Carpenter, a Unitarian Minister, and [163] member of the Association, but he was away in Manchester. I distributed about fifty copies of the Association's last prospectus among the principal Shopkeepers. I strolled about the ancient buildings in the Market Place. (the Barley Mow Inn; an old red stone building at the opposite corner of the Market Place) and several interesting specimens of antique wood and plaster houses with various latticed windows, projecting chambers and roofs with quaint old weather battered noseless faces ...

Waugh then begins an extended and fanciful description of the old architecture of Warrington which fills the rest of the page.

[164] I sauntered about the interesting old town musingly, till the time for the train to Manchester. I came away at half past seven. The night had cleared and was uncommonly fine and brilliantly lit by the moon. It was frosty and the air remarkably clear, and the cloudland was full of wild splendour and golden lights. The heavens above, and the green earth beneath were glorious to me that night! – Appearance of Newton and the surrounding country in the moonlight from the Legh Arms [?]

A calculation fills up much of the rest of the page.

TUESDAY 10 OCTOBER 1848. – canvassing for Subscriptions. Committee meeting in the evening. I am again writing from remembrance thirteen days after the time. I will be more punctual in the observance of my diary.

[165] *The page opens with another long calculation.*

MONDAY 23 OCTOBER 1848 – Resolved to write to Mallalieu tomorrow night. Went from Rochdale to Oldham by the nine o'clock train. Called upon Thomas Emmott at his factory behind the church. He had promised to assist me in canvassing for Subscriptions in the town today. He came out of the carding room all befluzzed from head to foot, with a short fustian jacket, and a cotton cap on. He shewed me into his little counting house, and asked me to wait till he washed his hands a bit, and put himself into fitter trim for the expedition. – We sallied forth and had good success, owing to his assistance. I have no time to say more now. I came to Manchester by the 3 ½ o'clock train.

TUESDAY, 24 OCTOBER, 1848. Wrote to Mallalieu. – Canvassed for subscriptions. – Committee Meeting.

[166] **WEDNESDAY 25 OCTOBER, 1848** – Wrote letter to the Examiner on the Educational Plan. Preparations for the soiree tomorrow evening.

'To do well that which before us lies in daily life, that is the prime wisdom.'

Essay on Natural Benefits common to all classes of Men. Take advantages which are free to all in the degree in which they are able perceive their value and their cheapness.

THURSDAY, 26TH OCTOBER, 1848. Preparations for the Soiree in the Evening. An assembly of highly intelligent men met at the Soiree. The Mayor, not particularly remarkable for either the clearness or the force of his reason, but Aldermen Kershaw and Sidebottom, Samuel Lucas, J. O. Dyer, Dr Watts, Dr Hodgson, Rd. Gardner, late M.P. for Leicester, Thomas Bazley, Wm Medcalf, and Rev Rd. Morris, and others who, though less gifted with speech were as rich in thought – deep and lucid thought – as any of them. – Dr. Hodgson's speech at the close of the meeting in reply to the objections of Kershaw and Medcalf set one on fire with emulation. – Forrest exasperated me with inconsiderate impertinence again tonight.

FRIDAY 27TH OCTOBER, 1848. – Copying letters to Literary Club [?] guests [?] who intend to visit the Athenaum Soiree on the 15th Nov. – I am unusually confused in brain today, and dissatisfied with the transactions of the day. I am wanting in energy and fixity of attention in the comprehension of daily business.

[167] *The page begins with a multiplication table.*

SATURDAY, 28 OCTOBER, 1848 Resolved to write to the Examiner tomorrow. – Went to Rochdale at night by way of Middleton. – Foxholes Lodge. –

SUNDAY, 29TH. – A miserable day to me today, except 3 hours in the afternoon with Crossley, Daly, Howarth, Mallalieu.

MONDAY, 30TH. – To Manch by 1st cheap train at 9[?] o'clock. – Sad reflections. – 'The girl I left behind me.' – Canvassing for Subscriptions. –

A weary painful day. * * *

TUESDAY, 31ST. – [*Entry begins with crossings out*] Writing report of soiree for the Papers. – Exam and Guardian. – Meeting of the Executive. – Dr. Davidson, Rd Gardner. – Our honorary Secretary is a downright humbug.

SUNDAY, 5TH OF NOVR 1848. – Dragged my disturbed heart about Foxholes Lodge till the afternoon. Oh unhappy marriage, thou paragon of damnation [*'earthly distress' has been crossed out*]. Went to seek the house at Lower-place, where the Texian Pilgrims – the philosophic brotherhood have appointed. – didn't know the house. – Listened at the doors to hear [168] some familiar sound that would guide me to the spot. – I heard my bluff old wrangling friend Mallalieu talking as usual. I walked in and took my seat among them. – Texas – the Existence of God – Sound – The character of the Bible as a School Book – Milton's Paradise Lost – Cameron's remarks on the Bible and Milton, – Walk to Milnrow in the Moonlight. Warm ale and rum at the sign of [*a space here*].

John Clegg's the Grocer, –

My wife at Lower Shore among her enemies. The unwise gush of my heart's hot bitterness at Clegg's – 'For all these things thou shalt be brought to judgement.' – Clegg invited me to Ale and Bread and Cheese – Eat [*sic*] a little more ale and rum with less stomach. – Took the road to Lower Shore by the Canal side. – The night beautiful but my heart strings all jangled. – when we reached Shore, it was past midnight, and all still, and silent except the sulky wind that skulked through the nooks and corners of the Old village, and crept through the dark bottoms between the hills with a slow moaning. – Sally knocked at the door of my wife's mother's, and called out, – 'Mary

Ann.' – She (my wife) answered from the inside, and got up, and her mother arose too, swearing and ripping and tearing, that she should not go out of the house, and pelting us through the lock-hole with the coarsest and bitterest epithets that she could pick out of her [169] rough dictionary. – The remembrance of the brutal insults, and the persevering malignity with which she had pursued me, ever since before my marriage, and the manner in which my wife, – knowing all this, and knowing also that it was without any conceivable cause of mine and how oft her mother had sought opportunities to get her to leave me – still persevered in going to her, against my desire; because I knew that she was not so much my enemy as she was and had been the enemy of her own children from their earliest age, – the great blight of their lives – and had sworn in her savage malice to let us have no rest till things were driven to the worst between my wife and me, – all this was in my mind and some of my blood rose with it. – I have often been at a loss to account for this fiendish virulence. I would at least have defied her evil intentions by keeping out of her way, which I never had wish nor occasion to get into. But my wife would not, and, in this respect, leagued with her relatives to destroy my peace of mind and her own, and to root up all confidence and love between us. – that night, when she began to spew out a filthy repetition of her disgusting devilment, I felt so exasperated that I began to emulate her in the same line. My wife came out, and I felt really embittered and disgusted with everything about me, her included. <u>High</u>, <u>low</u> words were vented which I am unhappy when I remember. – O God, for the heavenly heart of Christ! – My wife has an Aunt of the same blood, who lives 3 doors from her mother. – Hearing the riot in the still night, [170] she got up and came to the door 'in her shift un under-guot', and helped to swell the blackguard chorus. The wind stood still, and looked with astonishment on that disgraceful scene – Unhappy, despicable night-brawlers! – Miserable misery-breeders! The mother pulled my wife into the house, and locked the door, and swore she should not go out. – I shouted of 'Charlie', her brother, to send her out. She curst and swore, and opened the door again, and out came mother and daughter and son again all half-drest, one crying, and the other two cursing and swearing and blackguarding like devils. The mother shoved me off the door stones and knocked the Aunt (Sally) who had come up with me from the town clean down, and was hammering at her with all her heart till I took her off, and the son ran out in his shirt and ran his mother into the house again by the shoulder, with now and then a welt from his fist. – It was altogether a piece of hell's delight. – The Aunt (Mally) who lived close by came out of bed again, and opening her door, by the side of which we stood, she called my wife in and I followed after. She opened out her budget ['of blackguard talk' crossed out] ill stored with the same weary wares as we had too much of already, and she laid them about me without stint or hin.[8] 'Uv hoo'd a fella like me, hoo node damn'd weel how hoo'd fettle him.' – 'Hoo'd [171] match him damn'd sure othur o'one shap or onother.' But it boots not to repeat the foul mouthing of that night. I spoke with bitterness and coarseness that I am ashamed to think of myself. – The old man at Shore alehouse. – When my wife had got ready, we started for the town about 3 o'clock in the morning. She cried all the way –, but whether for leaving her mother, or for going with me, or because she was starved and ill, or unhappy in mind about the past or the future, I could not tell. – I felt too full of hot, unhappy distractions then to feel sorry for her, or, at least to manifest it to any degree. – I was mad against her, and spoke to her in the scorn and madness of my heart. But now that I am calmer, I am heartily sorry for her, and should like to forgive her and befriend her, – if I knew how, – and be forgiven by God and her for any of the harsh ebullitions of my unhappy heart. I cannot but blame her, especially in some moods of my mind with great bitterness. I cannot but blame myself too for allowing my poor temper to be so over-done, and my whole demeanor [sic] so warped from stern propriety by anything, – the worst that can befal [sic] me. – But in my calmest best moods, I see cause for charitable consideration both of myself and her. – O divine charity! How scarce thou art! –

[172] *A strange and unhappy period intervened here.*

TUESDAY 14 NOVEMBER 1848. Went to see Anderson's play 'Othello' at the Queen's Theatre. A most pitiful story. A dismally touching tale! Sad Desdemona and the noble-hearted moor! A tale full of beauty and heart-touching sorrow!

> 'Pale as thy smock my girl'
> ' When it shall ???

---

[8] i.e. without let or hindrance

O heavenly Father! Fill me with charity and love! O reform and purify my heart! O my only Friend sustain me! Bless me my Father and bless my poor dear girl O fill my heart with penitence and a forgiving spirit!

A long line at this point.

The period between this and the date when I next commenced writing was filled with the deepest distress of mind I ever experienced. – A weight of misery from the presence of which I shall never be able to rise up again completely. – My son born. – My wife's separation from at last effected by her hell-instigated relations.

Edwin Waugh,
the successful writer, in 1861.
In his left hand is a snuff box
by report belonging originally to
Robert Burns.
Courtesy of John B. Taylor.

Foxholes near Rochdale.
Engraving by J. Harwood and J. Davies, 1836.

The railway at Littleborough, 1845.
Tait Lithograph, courtesy of Science and Society Picture Library.

View of the Railway Station, Rochdale, 1845.
Tait Lithograph, courtesy of Science and Society Picture Library.

Manchester Victoria Station, 1848.
Tait Lithograph, courtesy of Science and Society Picture Library.

King William IV in Upper Shore. The date stone above the door shows 1792.
Photograph John Arnison.

The Caldermoor Inn.
In Waugh's time this was The Dog and Partridge, referred to in the diary.
Photograph John Arnison.

Holy Trinity Church Littleborough. There have been considerable changes, including a
new steeple, since Edwin Waugh attended services here in 1847.
Photograph John Arnison.

1849 (1)

[173] *After two blank pages the diary resumes in May 1849 with a letter to Joshua Butterworth:*

Potter Street
Hulme
Manchester

Dear Sir,

In your last letter to me you ask if I have entirely forgotten your letter to me on the subject of Scripture Extracts for the purpose of Public Education. – I have not forgotten it, although I have not replied to it. My path [*'life' crossed out*] has been so unusually beset with complicated business, and strange unpleasantness that my whole thoughts have been constrained another way, but the first opportunity I have of doing it effectually, I shall take some pleasure in writing to you again upon the subject. Meanwhile I hope you will remember me in your prayers, for I have need of prayers that avail more than I dare hope mine own to do

 Yours with a disturbed heart
 Mr Josh Butterworth   Edwin Waugh

Another page is then blank. Only the odd pages are written on until page 182, and, until page 181 the odd pages are much narrower. Whatever the turmoil of his private life, Waugh now seems far more confident about his job as Assistant Secretary of the Lancashire Public Schools Association.

[175] **FRIDAY, 6 JULY** – Visited the Secretaries of the Ardwick and Chorlton Districts, – and the Sec of the Strangeways District. Gave Strangeways a push. – Henry Taylor a dilatory fop. He will not do long. – I must relieve him of his onerous duties [*'as soon as politic' inserted*]. The office of sec must not be made into a 'fool's paradise.' – James Haughton, languid and unconcerned about the business. – to go. – No enthusiasm nor tact. – might as well send papers to Pendle Hill as to him. – Hackney a good fellow, but rather slack, wants support in his district. [177] Must get him some. – Visited Rev Tucker, and Rev Wm McKerrow about the coming farewell Tea Party to Rev Rd Morris. 'O, my prophetic soul!' The unholy cant which

will be uttered at that board-side! – Got some Subscriptions on my way home. –Wrote to some of the Div. Secs. to send in their Lists of Subscriptions. – Prepared for a campaign in Rochdale tomorrow. Went [*word missing*] the woman for my new shirt. Not finished. – She promised to bring [*page 178 is blank*] [179] it washed, at 10 o'clock to Scott's. – Dry toast, tea, and strawberries – The Bolton couple. – Matrimonial follies. – The company in Scott's Smoke Room. – These damned conceited tee-total asses! – Had a long conversation with the Rev T. E. Pointer of Patricroft – A scholar and a gentleman. – Went to bed glad that I had met with him.

[181] **MONDAY 16TH JULY, 1849** – Left Rochdale by the ½ past 10 train, with a heart heavily-luggaged with sorrow. – My poor Mary Ann! – She is handsome and weakly trained in mind, – She is away from me, and I am racked with doubts and miserable apprehensions. – She is in the hands of her relatives, who are of the most ignorant sort, and withal have a most virulent and unaccountable hatred towards me. – I am convinced that they would make any wretched sacrifice to satisfy their spite against me. – They have, unhappily succeeded in their determination to separate us, and to bring things 'to th'worst' between us. – Her mother swore to do it, and she will never rest till it is accomplished as far as possible. God, only, knows what the end of it is to be. – My poor girl! – What can I do? Her relatives have turned the world upside down to do me all the injury they can. They have importuned my employers with blackguard, slanderous speeches for the purpose of getting me turned from my employ. They have spread the foulest, foulest reports respecting me to do me injury. Their hellish intentions have so wrought upon my wife that [182] she, too, grows credulous, and has used me so unfeelingly that, for a while past, it has embittered my manners towards her, and long and severe provocation from all quarters, has made me speak things in the heat of impetuous bitterness, that were painful for her to hear, and for me to remember. All my past experience of sorrow is holiday-fun to this. – It is not for myself, but for her that I mourn. I could do well alone, if I had never known, never loved her. – but, now, come what will, she will be a life-long care to me. – O, my poor girl! – Never did woman's sweet smile play with such becoming witchery ['*on human face*' *inserted*] as on thine, my [*here are crossings out*]! I am jealous as hell, too. – O, the misery!

'I doat, yet doubt, suspect, yet
strongly love.'

How writing calms my troubled feelings! Shilly-shallied about the
office all day, quite irreconcilable to any thing but sad broodings. –
Espinasse gave me a copy of his pamphlet on 'Lancashire Industrialism'
– He and I went to the Café in Cross Street and took tea there. Bowker,
the Miles Platting [183] Secretary had promised to call at the Office for
us at 7, and go with us up to the Miles Platting Mechanics' Institution
where Espinasse was to lecture on 'The Education of Lancashire'. – We
left the lad in the Office to tell B to wait for us till we returned from
the Café. When we got back B had not been, and we set off to M.P
without him. – Called to see Rigby, – Chairman of the Working
Mens' Com in M.P. district. – He still very ill with inflammation
of the eyes. – When we got to the M.P. Mec.Inst, found it engaged
up to ¼ to 9 with a Tee-total Meeting. – Espinasse nervous, fidgety,
and annoyed. – We sallied out loungingly to see the habitations and
manners, and appearances of the dwellers in Miles Platting. – Espinasse
in a sadly sensitive mood, but still taking heedful note of all he saw,
and drawing some surface-diversion therefrom. As for me, my tongue
was far livelier than my head, which was away with my wife and child.
– We walked slowly back to the Institution, just at the appointed time.
Bowker ushered us thro' a side-door onto the Platform. I was requested
to take the chair, and at it Esp. went without let or hindrance. [184]
He enunciated his lecture (which he read) distinctly and clearly. The
audience chiefly dull-looking and uneducated factory-workers. I could
not with all the discernment I could put into mine eyes' search, imagine
more than some half dozen of the listeners before me on whose ears'
drum that suggestive lecture would not die away. – At the end of the
lecture I said a few words complimentary to my friend on his excellent
paper, and impressing its suggestions upon the hearers. Bowker moved
and somebody 2nded thanks to him, I put it, and it was 'signified in
the usual way' that he was entitled to the unanimous approbation of
the meeting, which broke up immediately after Bowker had told the
people that persons were at [sic] the names and subscriptions of those
persons who were willing to enrol themselves as Members of the Lanc.
Pub. Sch. Association.
    A knot of men like handloom-loom weavers staid in one corner of
the lecture room, and began to sing some old Wesleyan hymn tunes 'by

prick'.[1] Espinasse was delighted with the singing, especially with one tune, which, as he said, had 'a smack of Bacchanalian jollity in it.' He joined in with a [185] not unmusical, disorderly, rolling sort of rumble. I, too, felt a sad delight in the music. The tunes brought all my childhood to my memory. – My poor mother, and all her early struggles thro' poverty and obscurity, the hymns and the lessons she taught me. Bowker showed us thro' the building, – the Library, and the different schoolrooms – altogether, considering the difference of population, a better stored and accommodated institution than the famous one in Cooper Street. – Bowker invited us to supper at his house. – He kept a little Chartist publication shop in Oldham Road. The house had a rather dirty look. Expected something better than that, – more cleanly and tasteful from a man with so much common sense in him. – But that department depends upon the wife, I suppose, – and women who have been trained up to work in factories, and other like places during the day from an early age, do not often make clever, cleanly, housewives. Nevertheless, she was rather good-looking, and had a pleasant sensible expression [186] in her countenance. She laid new milk and bread and butter before us in abundance, of which, especially the milk, which was very good, we partook. Bowker then shewed us the invariable ornaments of most working mens' houses in this neighbourhood – certain portraits of Chartist leaders, O'Connell, Hunt, Williams, and Jones, The Chartist Convention, O'Connor, and the like. – These are often accompanied with a picture of Robert Owen, and some of his publications. He then took us into his cellar, – a dirty, stinking hole, where he had a host of fine rabbits of the lop-eared and other kinds, pent up in wooden runs. We sat and chatted a while till a whole battallion [*sic*] of little fat, Bowker infantry had been sent to billet ['*bed*' *crossed out*] by the Commander-in-Chief, and then took leave, sauntering homeward, commenting on the events of the day. – I parted with 'Diogenes' by the Palatine, and then sat up with Scott till midnight. – Fell asleep with the candle burning on the bed. Never mind. – I am immortal till my time comes.

[187] **TUESDAY, 17 JULY.** – Got in some old Subscriptions. Wrote to Emmott concerning canvass in Oldham. – Ordered the Charwoman to make me a new flannel shirt. My foot so swelled with wearing a tight boot, – one of the pair I bought in Smithfield for 4/3 – that I am forced

---

[1] By musical notation, not improvised.

to shuffle about in slippers till it gets right. – Committee Meeting. Reported progress of the districts to the Executive Com. – Had a glass of ale and a smoke with 'Dio' at the Roe Buck in Strangeways. – Loose talk with Scott and his wife, and a traveller in Scott's Smoke Room. – Went to bed late again. – My poor wife, – my Mary Ann!

WEDNESDAY 18TH JULY. – Very ill this morning. Wrote to Wm Heywood, Geo Adcroft and James Daly respecting Sub. Lists outstanding. Sauntered languidly about, feeling unfit for any common exertion. Got Sub. From N. Ridgway, the Gas Fitter, and from James Leslie, who wished me to put down his sovereign in the subs as 'money found' – not wishing his name to appear in the list publicly, since he subscribed also to [188] the opposition party, and, I think, is in some dependent position to some of them. I am very lonely, and miserable again today.

> Blithe summer's smile is cheering
> > Everything with glee
> Life to all life endearing
> > With fruit and melody
> > > But me.

> What boots this pleasant changing
> > In nature's witchery,
> To a lonely ['*mournful*' *crossed out*] pilgrim ranging
> > A heart enwintered way
> > > Like me.

> She need not spread her beauty
> > There's no enchantment in it
> To such sad smilers once a day ['*sorrowers every*' *deleted*]
> And sorrowers ['*mourners*' *crossed out*] ev'ry minute
> > > As me.

Resolved to take no snuff for a week from this day.

> And when smiles deck my feature
> > O do not think it mirth,
> There is no living creature,
> > With a sadder heart on earth.
> > > Than me.

[189] **THURSDAY, 19 JULY** – *The entry opens with more self-flagellation then …*

So far as occupation goes, I am never so happy as when I am writing. And yet, in prose and rhyme I am no more than an insignificant and obscure scrawler. I have, nevertheless, a restless, constitutional ambition to do something fit for the light, and for the good of the world in this way before I quit it. [190] Wrote to my mother, and Uncle Bob about the Rocking Chair. – Poor Mary Ann! – First and last, and middle of all my thoughts. What shall we do? O, my unhappy brain and heart, what shall I do for her? How can I save her? Damnation serve the fiendish mother who has brought this misery ['*between, upon both*' *crossed out*] us!

Long underlining here.

Sat up till ½ past 12 with Scott and a commercial traveller, – a jovial fellow, – talking with feelings in which deep glee, sadness, and love played strangely into one another, about Robert Burns! – Got my chest of books and papers from the house in Hulme. – Carried it up into my bedroom in Smithy Door, and felt more at home there. – Poor Mary Ann!

[191] *Much of the page is taken up with a heavily corrected and crossed out four verse poem. Significantly it is in dialect concerned with Waugh's failings, and showing Waugh working out how to represent dialect in writing. The last three verses are decipherable as:*

> They've such o' rook o' snip;
> They've moor nor au con do.
> If au're oles o' my shins
> They've wark oneuch for two.
> But, now aw think on't, Jem,
>
> Thea's plenty o' thy own,
> By th' mas, thea'rt war nor me;
> Pray for thysel' owd mon!
>
> And let mo ta' my choance,
> Aw'll ston it hit or miss;
> Aw cunnut think ut hell
> Cun be mich war nur this.

FRIDAY, 20 JULY. – Rose from a restless bed at six o'clock, a most unusual hour for me to rise at. – Strolled out in the still of the morning, – the air fresh and the sun shining. – My thoughts [192] held a parley with those quaint reliques of 'Old Mancunium' – the wood and plaster houses in Smithy Door and Old Millgate, and the neighbourhood – the Bull's Head where 'Bonnie Prince Charlie' took up his quarters when the Highland Rebels entered Manchester in the last Scotch Rebellion. – Strolled out among the fish-folk who were unloading their fresh cargoes with infinite bustle and noise – (there was a large majority of sturdy, hard-featured women among them thickly-clad in blue woollen petticoats and red-gowns, many with short pipes in their mouths,) – in the front of old Fox Inn, kept by Holden, a Preston man. – I sent Ann to by [*sic*] a trout for my breakfast. – She bought a beauty – ½ lb weight 4d – Felt fatigued and ill all day. [193] These two miserable years have played the devil with me. – It will take five as angelic as they have been hellish, to set me right again. –

Waugh goes on to tell how he was 'so ill that he was forced to lie down nearly the whole day' but consoled himself by reading 'Don Quixote' [194].

[195] **SATURDAY 21 JULY** – I am going to Rochdale again this morning … [*More self pity …*] Left Manch by the ¼ past 10 train to R'dale. Went to Fox Holes with Sally's umbrella, un th' key o' th Wayter Warks, which ad takin I' my pocket in o' mistake. Stretched mo cowt o' th'couch cheer o'while. – Greadly tire't fro head to foot, – inside un owt. – (It takes too much time to go on in this dialect-representing, – I must get on) – I slept a while. – When I awoke, all the hellish remembrances of the place began as usual to work upon my mind with excruciating power. – My distress grew so that I left the place and went to my mother. Grew calmer and <u>rested</u> there a while. – Walked thro' the town in the cool of the evening. – Called at my sister Ann's, – just because I must be moving about somewhere to break [196] the weight that presses on me in these unhappy fits. – Called at my Uncle Bob's, the hand-loom weaver. – He is like most of our family on the mother's side, – a musician – well known in the town and the neighbourhood, as a leader of singing choirs, especially among the Wesleyans. – I got 'o cup o' tay' wi' him an 'bullock' t' him o'bit obewt his lung-faced, lung-tong'd religious profession. – Spurious sanctity. After I had trotted him to the edge, I walked down to the town with him. – He continually

talking of his son Thomas, and wishing that he could get him some situation in a warehouse, or a respectable office where he could be drilled into writing and bookkeeping, and 'business habits.' – Went up to 'Th'Milkstone Lone' to see Jem Daly. – He just returned from a 3 weeks' sojourn in Ireland. – I thought he gave but a meagre account of his trip. – He had brought a good accordion back with him, cost him 12/- in [197] Dublin. – I <u>amused</u> myself (in the mournful way that runs thro' all I do just now) with tugging doleful noises out of it. Broken-backed voluntaries, full of distrest semitones, and discordant attempts at wailing. Home to my mother's last thing at night. – Read a few pages of the history of my dear old Don and his Sancho, while she cooked me a bit of steak on the grid which I eat [sic] ['nay, not the grid' inserted] with great relish to some hard oat cake and some small beer. – Went to bed late. – Saw my copy of Campagner Heal[?] lying on a chair. It reminded me of my last bed, to which I begin to look with more love than fear. – Good night.

SUNDAY, 22 – Was waked in the morning by a great pattering of water from all parts of the roof of the cellar where my mother lives. – A most unaccountable deluge! All fair in the open air, – the water falling fast in the house. – Drest myself and went into the street to keep out of the rain. – Came back, and, putting up an old umbrella, sat [198] in a corner, enjoying the music of the waterfall. – My mother bustling up and down, wondering wherever it came from. The stock of eatables did not take much covering, but I bounc't about helping her to cover all up. She ran up to the folks above. – The door was fast, and they fast enough, in bed. – The house was flooded, and water streaming out under all the doors, into the street. – The clogger and his wife got drowsily out of bed. – Hearing what was the matter, he curst and she scolded, and ran up and down the house half-drest. Cloggers' chips floating up and down. – a pigmy fleet, among which he splashed and jumped, and curst and swore like Neptune run mad. – The lads had gone out 4 hours previous, and left the tap running in the kitchen, and the vent in the sink covered up with a dishclout. – Leaving them scuttering and sputtering one over another, we put our share of the inundation to rights, and wiped it up [199] as well as we could, and I then got my breakfast with my mother very comfortably, and, stretching myself out on 3 chairs in a nook, with a pillow under my head, and lying there, and, now and then going out to smell the fresh air, I read

Don Quixote till near 4 o'clock in the Afternoon, to my great delight.
– Then thro' the town to Sister Ann's. – pint of ale and a smoke with
John Ashworth. – Went thence to Fox Holes. – The sad infection began
to work upon me immediately. – Poor Mary Ann! What will become of
her? She is mad, and I am distraught. Through the wood with her Aunt
Sally, ruminating sadly as I went. – Afterwards she went to Shore, and
I went with her on the way as far as Buckley. – Staid a few minutes
with Aunt Ann who lives with her husband and family in a comfortable
cottage there, with a nice bit of garden before the door. – They all [200]
with the exception of a son-in-law and his wife, – work in Scholefield's
Woollen Mill. – Scho is a kind of Manufacturing fuedal [*sic*] lord in
this little corner. – A griper, and a domineerer. – I never go down here
but they complain, on all sides, of the heaviness of their labor [*sic*], the
insecurity of employment, the insufficiency of their wages, and the overbearing manners of their employers. – Wages creeping gradually down,
even for heavier employment, and the chance of labor [*sic*] lessening.
– the housing and food and clothing of the operatives of this country
are fast sinking to the Irish standard. – They are stinted in everything
which is necessary for their welfare, except hard work, – which last is
dealt out upon the principle of too much or none at all. – As for their
minds and souls; – so long as they can weave flannel and spin cotton,
all else that enriches their possibilities [201] may go to hell for aught the
majority of their employers care. – The keenly-increasing competition
among master-manufacturers in this district, is driving them to try
to make up the difference to themselves by screwing more work, for
less wages out of the already over-wrought and under-paid operatives.
– The masters who feed and lodge sumptuously ['*well*' *deleted*] and are
comfortably clad out of the manufacturing system, cannot rid themselves
of a kind of compensating care that rides them continually. – They are
not happy <u>men</u>. – Where there is one that wrings much enjoyment out
of the gains of the system, it is, often, no more than a pig's parade to
him. – what these men gain in physical enjoyment they chiefly lose
in spiritual value. – Among the laborers [*sic*], – who live in fear and
trembling, from hand to mouth – there is a vast amount of physical
and mental suffering, which is, for the most part, unheard of. – [*Long
dash here*] Sally went on, alone, toward Shore. – I followed soon after,
going [202] by 'Th'Waytur Hease', th'Yeast Hill, Th'Starrin, Buckley,
Feathersta', Caldermoor, un Th'Turf Hease. – When I got a few yards

past Turf House, I saw a woman in a dark cap, with a white apron on, mending her pace towards me, and making signs of recognition to me. – Nearing a little, I was surprised to find it my wife, – so altered was she in countenance and dress. – She smiled the old enchanting smile, and I turned round to hide the delight it gave me, forgetting at the time, the way she has dealt towards me. – * * *. She asked me, hurriedly to go a farther off, as her mother was in sight, and if she happened to see me, a row would ensue. We walked on to Turf House, where she stept into a neighbour's house with me. – She knew the folks, I didn't. – For her own sake, I felt feelingly and forgivingly towards the girl who is so dear to me – my own wife, – the current of whose fate, whatever it is, will play anxiously about my heart while life lasts. I felt desirous [203] to make the best of what has fate or fortune has [*sic*] designed [?] to me, and help her to retrieve the errors of her early training, while I am equally desirous to amend those of mine own. – But my approaches were met again with that repulsive coarseness of deportment which she puts on so frequently to the utter damnation of all that is attractive in her appearance and disposition. – She demeaned herself towards me with an unfeeling rudeness that turned my stomach, and let loose her vituperative tongue [*'before folk' inserted*] in a way that disgusted me, and filled me with smothered indignation and sorrowful hopelessness. – she seemed hard and careless and as if she had no notion of having behaved in a way wrongfully to me. – To me that was a sickener. – what can I hope of her? I could smother all the vindictiveness which the manifold and unaccountable malignities of her relations and her own folly and want of feeling have awakened in my mind, and make my own aroused spite lie down, or go howling unsatisfied to its kennel for the dear sake of her welfare who is bound to me for life, but that the fact of her dead unconsciousness of misdeed, mixed with a kind of brazen, overbearing, affront [204] of manner towards me, forbids me to make any further concession (having even too much already, out of distress of mind on her account, besought her to me) to one so little conscious of the nature of the matrimonial contract, and who cast some bitter slights upon me, and then attempts to out-front them with an impudent demeanour. – O Mary Ann! Mary Ann! I wish thou wert as wise as I am proud. But

> I can stand and go
> Mourning to and fro
> Under as much woe

As any man I know,
And I must still do so,
Or make my bed full low.

A neighbour lass came running in to tell my wife that 'th'chilt wur cryin.' – She started out in a haste, without ceremony, as if I was no way considerable in the matter. – I followed her a few yards, and, with a heart full of unspoken madness, managed to ask her if she would come to me next week. She begun to make stipulations again, – [205] that I should give up my wages to her, and find her money to go back with, and the like. – The remembrance of the trouble I have had on her account, the way in which she has defied me and countenanced the injuries which her relations have attempted to do me, and her having run away from me – and to the place of all others which I desired her to keep from, – the way in which she has defied me wherever she has gone, rose in my mind and choked me with indignation. – Her appearance in a court of law against me, on her brother's behalf, – The christening her child without my knowledge, – and the whole unfeeling course of her behaviour to me – x x x x x x x.

I refused to give or send her any money for any purpose whilst she remained where she is. – She had found money for the purpose of leaving me, and she has put me to the great expence [sic] to me, of keeping a house waiting for her in Manchester, whilst, at the same time, [206] I have been compelled to live in lodgings elsewhere. – All this has put me to great expence [sic] out of small means – £1 a week, – and at a time when I find myself more embarrassed to meet the demands upon me than ever I was in my life. – I am more in debt than ever I was in my life. – I turned away, assuring her that this was the last visit I would make to her where she is. – I walked off, and she went the other way. – In a minute or two I heard her calling and running back to me. – She came to tell me that she would come to me, if I would send her money to come with. – I listened to her, and then walked on my way, determined to send her nothing of any kind nor to come near her any more so long as she thought proper to stay at her mothers. – I heard an old drunken stone-mason, known there abouts by the name of 'Jamie at th'Hill Top' staggering after me, and shouting to me to 'go obeawt thi bisnis, [207] we'n onoo like thee here.' – I took no notice of the stoitering old dotard, but went on down to th' Dog and Partridge at Caldermoor, formerly kept by a relative of my mother's (John Hurst). – As I went thitherwards, I passed by 'Midge Hole', the house where my mother lived – during the period of her first marriage, – with her [*first' deleted*] husband (James Hawkward). – They were well to do in the world, for working folks, – they made flannel for Newall's at the Hare hill – kept several pairs of hand looms for the purpose and employed workmen. – James was Newall's huntsman, and kept a pack of 'beagles' in a large kennel which stood on the opposite side of the road to the house 'Midge Hole' or 'Midge Hall' – I have heard all the folk hereabouts, who knew them well, say that my mother had the best furnished and cleanest house in all the country-side. – She was remarkable then, as she has ever been, for her industry [208] integrity and extreme love of order and cleanliness. – She was a remarkably good-looking woman in her youth. – I went into the parlour of the Dog and Partridge, hoping to find a quondam doctor there, who lives in the village below (Littleboro'). Last time I was at this house we had a cosy talk – interlarded with snuff and laughter, without stint, – about our different travels, he in Scotland and I in England, – He was not there. – I found 3 bull-headed country shopkeepers, and [*a lumpish-looking' inserted*] country lad drinking pints of ale in company there, and discussing the laws that affect 'Jerry Shops' and 'Owd Licenc't Heases' in the respect of admitting travellers to refresh themselves after 'th'sarvice time ov a Sunda.' Then the talk turned upon the swinish parson-magistrate at Littleboro' Chapel (Mills), and, so notorious is he for greed and guzzling, and general piggishness of life, that we joined in one chorus of condemnatory criticism of him. He was, it was unanimously agreed, – 'a wastrel o'gates.' – Then the trio of badgers discussed the prices of coffee, tea, and sugar, [209] and the comparative advantages of town and country trading in these articles, both to seller and to retail purchaser. – I sat and solaced my sick soul with a glass of brandy and water and a cigar, and, after that, and ballasting my stomach with cold mutton and 'cake brade' I went over to the other side, and, at their request, joined the quorum of fuddlers at their ale. – They treated me with a great deal of clumsy courtesy, and were particularly anxious to know who I was. – they seemed unwilling to believe that I was 'a Rachda' chap.' – A very disenchanting disclosure that to them. – Still they did not know me. – But, my being a native of Rochdale was a cooler. – 'A prophet has no honor [*sic*] in his own country.' – The rain was falling heavily, and the night was thick dark, which kept us later at the bench than I was inclined to, especially in my state of [210] of of [*sic*] health. – However, at ½ past 11 we broke up and I took the road towards Featherstall in company with one of the company, a young, noisy, senseless fellow, of the name of Midgeley, who keeps a small shop at Smallbridge, and is courting the daughter of Bamford, another shopkeeper at Lower Shore, which errand has brought the fool up to the neighbourhood, to win golden opinions of the thick-witted neighbours of his Dulcinea, by blustering and swillicking, and chucking his hard-earned money right and left, like sawdust. Small speech between us by the way, for I was ill, and he was witless. At Featherstall we stept into the Horse Shoe to get another glass of ale ostensibly, but really, he to show a hand full of silver, talk big, and deport himself altogether with a comical clownish attempt at free-and-easiness, – and I to rest myself a few minutes, watch him, and see what there was to be seen inside. – There was a [211] smell of burnt clothes in the house. – We found that their bed-room had somehow got on fire after the children had been put to bed, and some of the children's clothes, – one fustian jacket completely, – had been burnt, but the fire had been discovered, and put out, just in time to prevent harm to the little sleepers. – I was so ill, and the ale and smoke made me so sick that the talk that passed had little meaning for me. – We got up, and took the road in our hands again. – I parted with him at his door at Smo'Bridge, and dragged on to Haybrook. Where I turned up at Foxholes front gate, and through the grounds at the front of the house to Sally's Lodge. – Knocking loudly, I heard her get out of bed, and come down stairs, grumbling that she would 'put o' stop to their mak," she had 'said so mony o'time, but, bi th' [212] mass, this od bi th'last time.' – I knew she took it to be Charlie, her drunken nephew, who was at the door. – She opened, and I staggered in in the dark silently magnifying my tipsiness to preserve the disguise. – She called out 'Charlie'. – But I stumbled on, and spoke not. She then came and groped at my jacket, and found me out, and beckoned me to go up to bed without speaking, as her brother George, lay on the couch in the kitchen dosing [*sic*], ['*and*' *deleted*] he was no friend of mine in any sense. – I went up stairs noisily, and with a heavy, drunken foot, and I heard George say 'Is tat Charlie; he's mesterly drunken o'think.' – thea'm ta' care to waken him i'th'mornin', or else he'll be none up i'time.' – I went with willing bones to bed, and slept soundly till late in the morning. –

[213] **MONDAY, 23 JULY.** – I felt so unwell after last night's anxiety and indulgence that I was forced to keep my bed company nearly the

whole day. – Towards evening I turned out and visited my mother and afterwards went to William Hastings for his subscription, and thence to see Henry King, the Quaker, at Moss to see what I do with him [*sic*] in the way of inducing him to subscribe to our Association. He was not at home, but would be in before 9 at night. I learnt this of the servant who was milking in the Shippon. It was a lovely evening and I looked about me leisurely admiring the extreme cleanliness and comfort, and simple elegance of everything around the house of this opulent Quaker's [*'opulent' inserted*] father with whom he lived. The beautiful freshness of the green of the fields around, and the fine view of Blackstone edge, and the the [*sic*] hills towards Derbyshire. I strolled back to the town, across the Canal bridge, stopping a while to lean upon a gate and look over the fields where I used to walk with Mary. – O the heavenly remembrance! Walked about and mused a while in [214] the cool clear evening air. Went into the town again, and seeing Henry King going homeward I followed him at some distance, to give him time to get sat down, that I might make an effectual attack upon him. –I reached the house and found him in the Kitchen, sitting in a rocking-chair by the fire with a pair of hair slippers on, reading. – The maid was ironing a pile of snowy linen on the dresser. – I opened my business, by asking him, at once, to give a subscription to our Association, and the impression his face made upon me, led me, at once to tell him the sums which his acquaintances had contributed as the likeliest way to induce him to subscribe himself. He hesitated, looked blank, and, as I went on with my explanations of the principles of the Association, mingled with information respecting the progress and prospects and the names and amounts of the best subscriptions, I watched him tightly and [215] saw a 'swither' playing in his face, whether to subscribe or not, and then he would suddenly go red, and start at the thought of the awful sacrifice he was well-nigh making, and buttoning up his pocket, would say 'I think thou mun excuse me.' I, nevertheless, seeing the irresolution, and half-wittedness of his manner, pushed on vigorously, much further than I could have done with a man less rich, and less afflicted with the cramp in the fist than this was. – but it was no use, – no blood to be had from a stone thought I, and left him, rather ashamed of the degree of importunity I had used. – Went home and read Don Quixote.

TUESDAY 24 JULY – Went to Manchester by the ½ past 10 train. – Lounging in the Office all day, unfit for any useful turn. Committee

Meeting in the evening. – Smoke and a glass with Espinasse. – Got leave for a few days holiday!

[216] **WEDNESDAY, 25TH JULY, 1849** – Went over to Oldham by the ¼ past 9 train to meet Emmott, by previous appointment. We had to canvass together there. He was not at his mill at the time appointed, so I walked down to see James Hall at the Hartford Iron Works, and got his sub of a guinea … Pressed him for more. No go. – Went back for Emmott. – Caught him. – He invited me to dinner at his father's. His father is the Manager of the Oldham Gas works and has an excellent house behind the works prettily situated on a slope with a pleasant look out upon the green fields and hills for a long distance. There is a little green vale just behind the house, through which a brook rimples its wandering way. – I was pleased with the simple courtesy of Emmott and his two sisters at dinner, one of whom has a graceful figure and deportment, and such feminine sweetness in her face and manners, and a light in her eyes that I shall not soon lose sight of! – Heaven bless that [217] [*Phrase deleted ends with 'angel quakress!'*] [*sic*] I was rather amused, internally with phraseology of the family. Edwin, dost thou smoke? We have cigars in the house. – Dost thou prefer porter to dinner. The family are abstainers from intoxicating drinks themselves, and I felt the winsomeness of this uncommon politeness (uncommon for [*'professing' inserted*] tee totallers, who are, as far as I have seen them, upon the whole, rather an ungraceful and repulsive brood), in providing the means for their guests to enjoy [?] themselves in accordance with their own habits and opinions. – after dinner I tried their cigars, and we had a long conversation respecting the respective merits of the literature of fact and the literature of fiction. – They rather hastily condemned all works of fiction. I asked their opinion respecting the book of Revelations, Solomon's Song, Paradise Lost, and the Pilgrim's Progress and Spenser's Fairy Queen. – The young ladies happened to be embroidering some beautiful flower-work upon a mat. – I asked why they were taking such pains to engraft those [218] false roses upon their cloth. We had some pleasant talk about it. I tried their 'mild cigars'. – We next turned to the question of amusement, singing and dancing. – I asked what they thought of old King David's dancing and harping. – What of the songs of birds? What of the universal disposition of all young animals to express their emotions of delight in cries of joy, and limb-frolic? – – – The brother pointed out to me a patch of land,

7 acres in extent, in the shape of an L, which a number of unemployed Oldham cotton-spinners, with more energy, insight, and means than the rest, had taken from a neighbouring proprietor, at a rental of £ [*no figure is legible*] an acre, and cultivated it till it now produced the finest crops and kinds of garden stuff in all the country side. The occupiers had an equal division of the profits, after payments of rent, wages, and other expenses. – The intent of the scheme was to find employment [219] upon the land, for such of their number as happened to be out of work. – They were employed 3 days a week, at 2/6 a day. – This kept the wolf from the door, and they had all their garden stuff from the common garden, at a great advantage, besides that all profits arising from their purchases, and from their labor [*sic*] flowed back into their own hands. – It was really in fine condition, and altogether reflected credit upon the men who had devised the scheme and entered upon the land. – It is a wholesome hint [?] to the toilers of this country! I wish them, and all such, success! – Emmott and I left the house, and went on our way to do a bit of cadging. We went to Elkanah Moss's Mill at Greenacres Moor. – and to another Cotton Mill. – As we went he explained some of the technicalities of Cotton-spinning to me. – 840 yds, a hank of cotton – Counts – the number of hanks in a cop [220] We got Subscriptions amounting to nearly £6 and in the course of our Canvass, we had to call upon Eli Lee's, proprietor of the Soho Iron Works, the great roller making establishment. – Every process in this great works is effected by machinery from the pig iron to the finished roller, ready for the frame. – . – If Tubal Cain and his strikers were to rise from their dusty beds for a few minutes, and see the operations in this place, they would be struck dumb with wonderment. – Great hammers plying by machinery that shake the whole neighbourhood – blocks of iron cut through like so much cheese, and shavings planed off it as easily as off so much timber. – Leaving here, we returned to the town, and parted there, I going on, and calling upon a few other persons for their subscriptions, and he taking the road to his mill. Finding that I had done all I could for the day, and the evening wearing away, I went into an old, comfortable Inn, and got a Glass of excellent [221] ale, and a good beefsteak and some fine juicy onions. – I slept a few minutes on the couch, and then walked through the fields two miles to the Middleton Railway Station at Firs Wood, Chadderton. – Beautiful evening! – Took train to Rochdale. – Slept at my mother's. –

TUESDAY, 26TH JULY – To Manchester by the 8 o'clock train. – [*three words deleted*]. Squared my accounts, and left again at Noon for ten days holiday. – Query whether to go to the Isle of Man, or to Ireland, or to Durham to see little 'Robin'.[2] – Not money enough for long trips. – Must stop near home, among the hills, and be careful. – To Rochdale by the train at 3 ¼ – At my mothers [*sic*].

FRIDAY, 27TH JULY. – Took the train to Heywood to pay Heywood the printer the Association's a/c – Paid him. – Wrote to Espinasse – Called on Rev John Harrison, the Independent parson. – Had some talk with him about the Voluntary principle, and its [222] applicability to Public Education. – I maintained its inadequacy for the purposes of a really general '<u>national</u>' Education. – He maintained that the ['*application to Government for the*' *inserted*] enforcement of a Tax upon the whole people for Public Education, however unsectarian in its character, was a dangerous departure from the principles of popular independence. – I thought him a sophist. – Went to see Parry at his school. He is the Swedenborgian Minister. – He called the roll up of his bare-headed wiselings [?] in desultory style and dismist [*sic*] them – and then we went to dinner together. His late Master in the School had left and gone to the South of England. – And he was expecting another every day. – The lads thought I was the man, and as I went thro' the streets, I heard them say one to another, 'That's th'new M ['*e*' *deleted*]aster!' – Parry's house [223] is roomy and pleasantly situated for Heywood, but the interior betokens the stint of salary he labors [*sic*] under with his young family. – After dinner we sat and talked about the servility and dependence of Parsons generally, – a favorite [*sic*] theme with me – and a feeling one with him, for he knows the galling life of a poor dependent, dissenting parson. – However, he begun the subject so we rattled at it a while, without remorse, and he seemed mightily pleased with the talk. – After washing and shaving myself, we went out into his garden, – a large one in the front of the house. – It was very weedy, and altogether neglected, but, nevertheless, had some fine fruit trees in it. – We set to work, and eat [*sic*] an abundant dessert of the finest, currant berries, gooseberries, and strawberries, fresh [224]

---

[2] Before taking a job on the Wakefield Journal, Waugh had worked for two years on the Durham Chronicle (Robertson, 1881 p. 170). 'Little Robin' may possibly be a reference to an illegitimate child for whom he paid upkeep (Vicinus 1984 p. 14).

from the trees. Shortly after I walked on to Rochdale by Marland, after getting the little parson's subscription for 5/- to the Association. – Stopt at my mothers.

SATURDAY 28ᵀᴴ JULY – Staid in the house all day reading Don Quixote. Strolled thro' the town at night.

SUNDAY, 29ᵀᴴ JULY. – After breakfast went up to Daly's. I proposed a stroll to the hills. He accepted, and off we went, calling for Brierley, a young printer, by the way. – We sat down and waited until he got ready. – . – We took the road over Cronkey Shaw, and thro' Syke, Buckley Wood, Ridings, Wardle, between the Hills to Middle Wood, and Higher Shore. – Over the hill to High Lees. – Down by Rake Foot. – Daly and Brierley agreed to call and see Mary Anne [*sic*] and the little lad. – I stayed behind, waiting for their return at the end of [225] the New Mill. – They came not, and concluding that they had gone on to Rochdale, expecting to meet me on the road, I turned and went down to Turf House. I asked a farmer's wife, and acquaintance of hers, to slip up to the Calf Hey and privately let her know that I was at Turf House. – She, after a little hesitation, in which I read a little disinclination to meddle with the matter, folded her infant up in a shawl, and went her way to do my wish. – She returned in a few minutes, accompanied by my wife, who had the child in her arms. – The particulars of our interview, and how her mother came in after her, and made a blackguard uproar, will be found in my metallic Memorandum Book No.2 – – – Went down to Caldermoor, to the Dog and Partridge Inn. – Dr Barker sat grinning from ear to ear in the corner where I had mist him last Sunday, and we had [226] some talk about the Cholera, which is ravaging in some parts of some of our great towns,[3] and about Carrarra Water, and other drinks of that description which contain fixed air; and respecting snuff, which he takes every few minutes, out of a large silver snuff box. – An old gentleman of the name of Race, with a white head and benevolent look, came in and took his place quietly in the corner, which is always resigned to him by any who happen to sit in it at the time. He always leaves his tobacco in that corner, and it remains there for his own smoking, unmolested by all who come there.

---

[3] In fact there was a cholera epidemic in Manchester in 1849. It broke out in June and was 'prevalent' in September. (Axon, 1886, p. 250)

– Everybody in the house shewed him uncommon courtesy. – If his pipe went out, all in the room – doctor and all, – rose from their seats, and hastened to light a spell for him. – He couldn't bear much light, and the gas, for the especial pleasuring of this [227] white headed old favourite was kept unpleasantly low for everybody else, except so far as they took some delight in obliging him in every little thing that could shew their kind feeling towards him. I had told the landlord to get me some eggs and ham cooked, for I was sincerely hungry. He popt his head out the parlor [sic] to say that all was ready in another room. I went mealwards and ' played a good stick'. – Returning to the parlor, old Race asked my leave to ask me a saucy sort of question. – He wished to know whether I was a native of Rochdale, or not. – I thought he remembered my face. – I told him I was at present a resident in Manchester, altho' a native of Rochdale. I saw in the faces about me a disposition to know more. – my name and position, but, partly for mine own amusement, – partly because I wished to enjoy the deference which they paid to me unknown, which, had they known my name and humble origin, they might have denied me – and then, I did not wish my [228] errand into the neighbourhood to be known to everybody. – Perceiving that I did not wish to be more communicative, – altho' with evidently unabated curiosity, they pushed it no further. – Old Race and the doctor supt up, and departed, bidding me a respectful good night. In came two hearty middle-aged countrymen, and I began to talk with them about the cheapness of pure air and good water in this neighbourhood, and the numerous fine picturesque walks in it. – Our talk then turned upon filth in ['some' inserted] large towns which we had all seen. – They took snuff, and were social with it.

– this sprang the snuff question. – I told them the story of the origin of the name 'Irish Blackguard' for the snuff that bears it. – They were much amused by it. – They shortly supt up and went – and I followed into the moonlight, where I stood and mused a few minutes, with a cigar in my mouth. – I was debating whether to take the train at 20m. past 10, to Rochdale, or to walk there thro' Middle [229] Wood, and between the hills, or to call at 'King Bill's' at th' Shore. – The King won, and I took the road thither. – The night was fine, the air clear, and sweet with the new hay, and a few white straggling clouds sailing over the ['nearly' inserted] full moon. – I was pleased with every thing about me, and soothed in spirit. – Entering King Bill's kitchen, I found his majesty as drunk as a fiddler's bitch, sitting in his shirt sleeves on his usual throne, the couch before the fire, with his arms folded upon his knees, and his body bent, and shucking his head from side to side, with a drunk grin upon his face, and pouring out a stream of rough, drink-crazed humour, which I took a strange delight in listening to. – I got a glass of ale and a smoke, and, as the night was far spent, and I tolerably comfortable where I was, and near where I had promised to be in the morning (for I had forgotten to say that, when my wife's mother came upon us at Turf [230] House, and assailed us with a host of comical names, such as 'bull-yeded wastrel', and 'blash-boggart' and the like, Mary Ann had whispered that she would meet me at th' 'Co'do' Moor Ale Hease', at Eleven o'clock in the forenoon of the following day) – I determined to stay all night where I was, if possible. – The buxom landlady said I might, after making a host of apologies about the greatest part of their bedding having gone to the 'whitsters', and if I had no objection to sleep with a young man who lodged with them – an overlooker in the neighbouring mill. – All right, and I off to bed, and slept not the soundest because of too much smoke and ale I had indulged in.

MONDAY, 30 JULY. – Up at 7. – Pretty view of the fields, the railway, and the Dale of the Roch out of the little window towards 'Starrin' – Fine wash in the big tub at the back door, enjoyed the cold morning air, that whistled thro' the 'ginnel' – Fine view of Middle Wood and the meadows, from the back door. – King Bill [231] stoitered down to breakfast at 8 as drunk as when he went to bed. – Drink had been his only meat and solace for a whole fortnight, and they who knew him well said he had not yet reached the culmination of his fuddle, and would very likely be a fortnight, after he 'took up' as they said, in waning back again into that state which they called his 'soberness', which was a kind of sour, speechless, remorseful, nervous melancholy, – a condition which was more feared by the inmates of the house than the worst moments of his drunken bouts, in which he was commonly a tolerably peaceful and very humours [sic] companion at the pot, and a great attraction to the folks on [sic] the country side who like fire side fun and a glass of good ale. – But, before he reached this miserable crazy sobriety, he had to wade thro' many long nights and days, palpably thick to him, with infernal horrors of [232] all descriptions, and devils of all the colors [sic] of the rainbow, and of all shapes and sizes. He sometimes would fling money into every corner of the house, where he saw them, to buy himself off from their eager claws. – Poor King! – He was no sooner at the foot of the stairs, than, in a tremulous tone, he begged the Queen to 'shap him o'nice little un' by which he meant that she was to prepare him a glass. – She, knowing him well, readily served him to his heart's content. – He sat down on the couch, fuddlers began to drop in, the long dog was loosed from his kennel, the visitors who were staying in the house came down stairs, and the day's fun began. – I took to smoking cigars in a nook of the kitchen, and taking note of his curious marlocks and expressions – The Queen had a sister over from [233] Wakefield. – I chatted with her about that town and its people. – Up to the Moors in the middle of the forenoon to sniff the mountain wind, and look down upon the world for a while. – Through the 'Adder's Wood' and over the fields in a heavy shower to the Dog and Partridge at Caldermoor. – Got my dinner there. Waiting. – No [*go*' *deleted*] come. – What an ungraceful old devil M A's dam is! There never was one manufactured with less sense, more deceit and spite, – nor a rivener [?] – O, the unhappy day! – A hearty-looking country cobbler came in while I was at the Dog and Partridge, and after repeatedly showing me his best civilities, and inviting me to his ale, he asked me home to tea with him. – I was ready for aught, so I went, as much out of curiosity as anything else. – I found that 'Bill o'Franks' had a comfortable country homestead, and well stocked with [234] stomach-gear, and small, white-headed human cattle. His substantial, clean-looking wife, hustled about very good humouredly to make us both at home altho' we were both elevated above the top total standard. However, she knew how to wear the bridle upon herself that would check him best, and received us both, altho' I had never seen either before, with a good tempered country welcome. – We took our tea [*'which was real stinger, and I felt an old womanish love for it' inserted*], with a plenitude of fine white cakes and butter, and 'aft she prest and aft I ca'd it guid'. [*I felt dull but made the best attempt at grace and gratitude that I could muster' inserted*]. I noticed some simple lines done in needlework, and hung up in a frame against the wall. – They had been wrought by one of his little daughters, just under one of those comical, cotton-factory-looking 'exact representations of Solomon's temple' which one meets with so often, in needlework, in such houses – No more like what Solomon's temple was than 'four-and-nine' is like a [235] first-rate British Man-of-war. – The absurd herioglyphics [*sic*], and misrepresentations, and the numerous orthographical blunders met with so oft on children's sample-cloths wrought at school, bespeak the gross ignorance the greatest part of teachers of girls' schools, about the sample sewing age, – as I believe the qualifications of teachers of schools of all kinds and ages throughout the kingdom is greatly defective. – There is no sure test of the qualities of teachers. – It is evident that pupils cannot put the qualities of their teachers to the test, – and if they could, perhaps the inclination of youth generally would lead them to prefer to have it undone. And their ignorant parents are at the mercy of ignorant teachers, and too often deluded with the hope that their child is advancing in sound training and knowledge, whereas the child, often, gets nothing but the harsh restraint and [236] sickening buz [*sic*] of a few uninterested, ill-employed school-hours every day. – There is a good deal of 'obtaining money under false pretences', in the system and it must be so until the people generally are better awake to the requisites of a teacher, and the nature of good education, than they are now. – However, we are creeping on to something better, by and by. – Oh I took the trouble to write down the lines ['*which were sewn*' *inserted*] of the child's sampler as they call it. – I thought them simple expressions and more appropriate than many that I had seen on such things. –

> Our life is never at a stand,
>   'Tis like a fading flower,
> Death, which is always near at hand,
>   Comes nearer every hour.
>
> Children, that now are young and gay,
>   Like roses in their bloom,
> Will very soon be old and grey,
>   And wither in the tomb.

The above remarks about such needlework do not apply to these lines, – They were wrought correctly and with good taste.

[237] I returned to the King's in the evening. – His receipt for 'spackin' a wife.' – 'Providence a wise fellow.' – Meditations on the external and internal regimen necessary for the improvement of my health – Sat in Eliver Wood when the sun was sinking. – The calling of the cows home. – The hunting cries at the Dog and Partridge Inn. – Hey beauty! – Blossom Ho Blossom! – By! By! Ho, my little dogs!

Hey Bantam, little bitch! Come back yo' thieves! Come back yo' there! O'er a gate! O'er a gate! Ho dogs! Yo ho! Yo ho! –

Bright chanticleer proclaims the dawn!

Waugh then repeats these cries using a wavy line to indicate the rise and fall of pitch in the huntsmen's voices.

[238] King Bill's 'bit o' dangerous talk wi' his dog, Spring. – 'He nodded his yed ut every <u>point</u>, and sed he didn't care for aught ut te coud'n bring agen him'. – 'and bak him agen the devil or he'll come up.' – 'Aw seed o' rook ov his marlocks to-day, – by th'mass, he's a crumper.' – ' Mother, yo' mun keep or Sal in, th'millreets are comin' agen.' – 'Thear't wrong gated, – By goss, art to, too' – King B. to his dog. – His songs. –

> 'As Dolly sat milkin' her cow'
> 'You gen'rals all, and champions.'

I stretched myself out on the bench in the tap-room with Don Quixote under my head, and dozed while 'King Bill' sat, maundering, and swinging his head from one side to another, [239] and grumbling and swaggering about his dog and his wifes [*space left here*] and making ludicrous face, and attempt at singing

> 'It rains, it hails, it snows, it blows.'

The millwright's wife, and the Wakefield engraver's wife donned themselves up in their best, and went a-shopping to Littleboro' – They called at my wife's mothers, and told my wife not to come over to 'King Bills' till they returned, lest her mother should suspect her errand, – or, as the Wakefield dame said – for fear they should 'think it wur gillory.' – On their return, she came across with them, unsuspected and sat with me in a little room called 'The Snug' out of the way of eyes and noise. – We sat and talked, and I nursed the little lad. – I thought he looked delicate and thin. Poor little fellow [240] with the pretty face! – How innocent, helpless and engaging he looked! – Poor fellow, he will need great care to rear him. – We sat and talked about future movements in our affairs, – the child, his wants, – means of household accommodation, – house-gear, – income, – debts, and the like. – I was delighted to see her and the child. – while we were talking, and she had stayed longer than prudent, if the peace was to be kept by her virago of a mother, in ran the Yorkshire dame to say that my wife's mother was cleaving the wind to get at us, and would be in in an instant. – She has the tongue and temper of a born devil, and so, the news made us jump to shift. – But too late. – I, knowing what was in the wind, could not but laugh in anticipation of the coming scene, altho' it was anything but desirable. However, I drew up my legs [241] and 'hutched up' in the corner as well as I could, to elude her march, but it was no use. – She was on us in a minute, and opened her hellish battery upon us without stint or stop. – The Queen, the millwright's wife, the Yorkshire dame, and the servant came to stand between and

'moderate the rancour of her tongue.'

['But she' deleted] it was 'no go'. – She pelted at it, – ding dong, phit, phit, with her ten claws spread and set before my ['face' deleted] eyes, and then she fastened on the child to carry it off. – I lost my temper in an instant, and in the moment's exasperation, should have struck her if she had not let go, and the women stept in. – after the old wild, savage had gone on a few minutes more riving and raving, Mary Ann agreed to go [242] over home with her, and prepare her clothes to leave them. – We parted thus, and she and her mother, and the little lad left the house. – The women who were in the house followed, to ['make' deleted] negociate [sic] for a peace, if possible. – They stopt near an hour. – They returned, in a body, laughing and chattering like magpies, and assured me they had kept all quiet and right. – I, who knew the nature better than they, knew they were mistaken. – Hell's delight would commence as soon as they were clear of the house. – It turned out afterwards that I was right. –

Tom Holt, the millwright, a dull, sottish-looking, lumpishly-built man, sat by the little round table, looking very glum, and sulky, all the while the women were out of the house. – He rose and scratched his head, and pushed his ale [243] on one side with an hasty, disturbed air. I noted the change in him instantly, but it did not strike me just then what was the cause of it. – He begun to ask with an ill-concealed anxiety in his tone and look, where his wife was off to. – He was half drunk and looked mazier than common. – As oft as he asked, – perceiving the cause of his unhappy restlessness, – I tried to re-assure the poor devil by telling him that she was just over the road at my wife's mother [sic], and he, as often, answered me with a deeply-dissatisfied air – 'O well, hoo's <u>reet</u>, ov hoo's theer.' But the quiver in ['his' inserted] sour face revealed his internal convulsions. – I prest him to drink, but he put it aside, and with a clumsy gloom o'er-clouded, excused himself, – a strange sign in him. – At last he got up, hastily, and went to his bed without speaking; and I was left alone, thinking over the occurrences of the day. – When the women-folk, and all in the house were laughing and talking together, we heard the millwright get lumbering out of bed, and come thumping down stairs. – He came into the kitchen in his stocking-feet, and [244] with a face full of the dullest, drunkenest displeasure, and with one arm outstretched, and a clenched fist, ['*about the weight of a tailor's goose' inserted*] at the end of it. Looked silently at his wife for a minute, and then, seizing her by the hair, he struck her in the face. – The women screamed, and every body was struck with astonishment [*'It was soon perceived that the millwright was as jealous as hell' inserted*] X X X X X In a few minutes peace was restored, and though the neighbourhood around the wife's eye rose up big and black with the blow, and she look [*sic*] sulky at him a while, – the song was sent round from one end of the kitchen to the other, for the space of two hours, – soon after, all the inmates of the 'King Bill' were quietly at roost and at rest in their beds. –

'O bonksman ov o' ham'

Tale. – 'Th'Pendle Hill lions.'

'That man is never drunk,
No, never drunk
Who can dance Peter O'P' – March

King William's Song and march to shew that he was [*'still sober' deleted*] 'na fou'.

[245]   'Go to thy looms'

'Ston thy dogtchin'

'Jacksouring'

MONDAY, 6 AUG. – Staid in bed nearly the whole day at Foxholes Lodge. – Wrote to Espinasse to say that I was not able to come to Manchester till the following morning. – Waiting for Mary Ann. – At 4 o'clock I heard her come in at the front door, and call out 'Hallo!' I answered from above, 'Who's there?' 'Me' said she, in a pettish tone. – I knew who it was, before she spoke. – I donned my clothes, and went down to her. – It made me sad to see her looking so thin and ill. – Poor lass! – some talk. – She had left the child at Milnrow at her cousin's. – I would as lief she had left in hell [*sic*], except for its own [*'sweet'* inserted] sake, so completely do I dislike the impudent, ignorant woman who lives there, and the meddling, spiritless, sniveller her husband. [*'Damn 'em' deleted*] I shall [246] hate 'em both as long as I live. – Went thro' the fields with her to Milnrow. – Her anxiety about the child. – Walked about the village among the wakes wassailers thinking. – At last, could stand it no longer, and went into Clegg's to look at the lad. – Mary Ann prepared to go home with her Aunt and the child, when I went in, or there would soon have been nasty words between me and the overgrown sow, (Clegg's wife), in fact she commenced as soon as I went in, but I gave her a red-hot reply, and the folk bustled out with the child, which caused further blackguardism. – Walked up to Shore with the company. – Fine moonlight night! – King Bill's bower. – walk thro' the fields and by-gates to Foxholes. – Slept there. –

'Oh, what'll ta do wi' thy hond neaw.'

[247] **FRIDAY, 10 AUG** – Bought at John Lee's Upholsterer in King Street, – the following furniture,

French Bed
Mattress
4 chairs for Bedroom
One Arm Chair, made of Yew Tree
One Bedroom Table

Glass of ale, and walk to Higher Broughton with Espinasse. – After, walk towards Cheetham Hill with the Morris Dancers and Rush-Cart from Cheetham Hill Wakes. – Hey for country fun! – The green fields for me! – Ended the day with sad ruminations.

'A man's a man for a'that'
'Burns's Address.'
'The death of Nelson.'
The Burial of Sir John Moore.
The Battle of the Baltic

[248] **SATURDAY 11 AUGUST 1849.** Cheetham Hill Rush Cart and

Morris Dancers passed through several of the streets in the centre of the town, accompanied by a band of music. The day was uncommonly fine and the sight was a novel one in the streets of this busy city. Such a one has not been seen there for many years. It was a pleasant relic of an ancient festival, and gave an agreeable surprise to the inhabitants, and the merchants in the Exchange. – After dinner, I packed up my traps, and strolled into Shudehill till the time for the starting of the train. I passed Elijah Ridings' Stall. There he sat on a low stool at one end of it, with one leg over the other, [*'and' deleted*] his stockings down and the slop of [*'his' deleted*] the topmost leg of his trousers drawn up to near his knee, exposing a span's-length of a hairy shin. He was too deep in a book which he held in his hand to notice anything about him that did not make more noise than ordinary in that uncommonly noisy spot. – The state of his book stall, bespoke the poverty of his circumstances. About 20 dirty-looking books strewn disorderly upon a small, rickety-looking stall. – – –
[249]

An attempt at a poem in standard English follows concerning the 'Parnassian climber'. It ends

> *Be true to thyself for ever*
> *Be just, and take no fears.*

Took train to Rochdale at 6 ½ . – my mother. – Her advice. – Foxholes. – Oh the hell of conjugal unhappiness! Walk to Shore. – King Bill's. – Edmund Bamford's house, at Rake Foot.

[250] Tum we'll gie tho o' quart o'ale, I' thea'll come un level ir cheese up.

Mam awm beaun to th'Rushbearin, an aw think awst have o'woman, owm owd eneuch neaw. – Well aw care nought obeawt it, nobbut, mind ut to puts up at a greadly un. – Tum coom back at neet, un towd his mam, ut he getten o'woman un he'd come'd whoam wi' her. – Un hoo is her? Said th'owd lass. – 'Bet ut th'Grimes', said Tum. – Damn tho, didn't aw tell tho to have o'greadly woman', said hoo. –'Aw know that', said he, 'but aw mut e'en taw whot o could get,' – awd ha yo to know ut greadly women 'll ha greadly fellows.'

'Thea munnut expect no blozzums ut th'after this.' – Warning on Re-union

'Thea'rt o <u>write un poverty</u>.' Mary Ann's mother to me.

Thoughts on the mean entanglements of my heart.

The source of true authority, resolute will, and tranquillity of mind –

[251] 'That's o' <u>whot</u> un' – King Bill

King Bill's Yorshur Duck. – Anecdote

'Dunnot ta o'th'twist eot o'th'porritch.' – Anecdote

'Hasty wark's none good work.' Ned Bamford, o'th' Rakefoot.

Mary Ann came to Manchester on the 13th of August 1849, to the house in Ruby Street Hulme. – * *4

---

4 According to the Manchester Directories of the time, Waugh's address was 13 Ruby Street, Hulme.

1849 (2)

After this dramatic announcement follows a poem in standard English filling the rest of page 251 and the whole of page 252. Then, on page 253, Waugh writes down a history of events immediately before his time at 'King Bill's'. The entries appear in reverse chronological order, which seems to indicate his distressed state of mind. Moreover the first entries precede in date the original entries for 1849. He then recounts events after his time there, and especially the details of Mary Ann's return.

[253] Espinasse's anecdote of Carlyle. – 'The world is a poor slave and will always be governed in a low way.' – Carlyle speaking of Geo. Dawson said, 'Aye, he struck <u>twelve</u> all at once.'

I had written the following notes of days before this date on loose slips, and being unwilling to lose them, and wishing to have them in safer shape, I have taken the trouble to copy them in this lumber-book.

WED. 5 JULY [*actually the 4th*] – Wrote another letter to Mary Ann. – It is too sentimental and 'curious-good'. – I dare not send it. – She would not believe it nor understand it. – Perhaps she would take advantage of it. – O, my poor lass! – What can I do? I have been in hell all day! – Every thing in this disgusting town makes the thought of her doubly-miserable. – My heart is distracted with love, fear, doubt and indignation. – Went into Smithfield Market, and bought a second-hand pair of Wellington Boots for 4/3. – Thought the 3d. was put on take off again. – Haggled about it, for the fun of the thing. – No go. – Tight as wax. Hard work to get them on. – tugged and sweat, and stampt on the flags, till the folk [254] gathered round, some laughing at me as if I had been in the stocks, some grinning with me to help my boots on thereby. – So many came round that I invited them to give me a lift, just to see what they would do. – They came in such numbers – and helpt me in such clumsy earnest, that I was forced to invite them to drop it. – Went up to my lonely house, and donned my best trousers, and a pair of new socks. – Slept at Scott's. – Pleasant chat with him and his wife. – Made me sad at the thought of mine. – Smoked a pipe. – Read Milton till morning.

There follows a prayer.

Received a letter from the poetical Tinker who is sojourning at Matlock Bath in Derbyshire, and is running over with the inspiration that nature's loveliness diffuses into such hearts as his. – Wrote to him. – [255] He will probably be offended at my rough criticism of his style. – No matter. – Gave friend 'Spea', author of Solitary Musings' [*sic*], a job delivering circulars. – Poor scribbling fancy-monger. – Glad of any to get an honest penny for bread and cheese. – He was a short time since, a private in the 30th. Reg. of foot. – My mind full of mixed miseries of all sorts and sizes. Went to see 'Macbeth' at the Queen's. – Coffee and a smoke with company of the coldest-hearted, emptiest, conceitedst [*sic*] tee totallers I ever had the mischance to meet with. – slept at Scotts. – Wrote letter to Mary Ann – more to relieve the anguish of my mind than with the intent of sending it.

SUNDAY JULY 1. – Sat at Uncle Bob's, the weaver, eating, smoking, and writing notes. – Felt ill all over. – As we sat at breakfast Uncle Bob's anecdotes of my grandfather interested me exceedingly. – After dinner went to Foxholes. – Sally had much news from that little hell, – Lower Shore. – Disgraceful, disgusting, pitiful! – Lay down and slept 5 hours. Pondering how to condense my social relations, and bring my habits into some correct bearing. –

[256] **SATURDAY, 30 JUNE.** – Breakfast at Scotts. – 'Mad Jacob' the knavish, old, Smithy Door Bookseller,[5] strutting about the flags this morning, with a kind of a conical basket-hat on, with a bunch of shavings stuck on the top of it, for a feather, and shouting out 'by, by! by, by! – Put No 2 of the Edu. Reg. into the printer's hands. – Ordered Circulars and Tickets for the Rev R. Morris's Tea Party, and slip of printing for extensive distribution. – Got book, for check against District Secretaries. – Called on a few persons for their promised Subscriptions. – Went to our two working friends at the Examiner Office. – Wilkinson, a sensible fellow, active, intelligent, but lacks force. – France, generous but languid. – Neither of them had brought their Lists of Subscribers. – To have them on Monday. – On return to the Office, found little 'Diogenes' wrapt in creative mood, writing furiously and smoking. – He handed me a cigar, and begged me not to disturb him for a while. I sat, smoked, and read 'Paradise Lost' till 2 o'clock,

---

[5] This was the Smithy Door bookseller Jacob Williamson (Directory 1850).

then went and paid 'Uncle Jem', th'Arcade Book-monger his fourpence. – [257] Got shaved, and my hair cropt close to the floor of my skull. – Went into Shudehill, and got my shoes patched, while I sat on a crazy counter in my stockin' feet in the cobbler's cellar. – As I walked down the street, rejoicing my renovated understanding, a poor country-fellow's horse fell under a heavy load of coals; the tremendous weight of the shaft pressing on his fore legs, very painfully and dangerously. The poor fellow in great concern about his horse. Luckily, as is generally the case in these streets, – where such accidents happen often, – there was no scarcity of ready-witted, active men about such matters, who laid hold of the horse's head, loosed his trappings, raised the shafts, turned the cart and load, got the horse up, rubbed him down, walked him about in the air a few minutes, gave him a drink, and all was right. – I was handsomely daubed with cart-fat, and walked through the streets with my fingers spread out as frozen as the hand of a wax doll. – Took tea at Scott's. – Disgusted with the ignorant brag, vanity, and fanaticism of the Tee-total spouters that swarm about here. [258] – O, for a little quiet seclusion, occasionally, in this damned sickening world. – Means to Ends. – Train at 6 to Rochdale. – Saw Cousin Jack in one of the Carriages. – He told me that Beckett Smith Esq. of London, who 40 years since borrowed about £1000 from my Aunt Jane, and proved insolvent afterwards, had, in the course of the meanwhile, turned out one in a hundred, – an honest man. – He had sent over a considerable instalment of the borrowed sum. –

Visited the Co-operative Store in Toad Lane. – Jem Daly, Sec. – This Association is creating a great sensation among the working people. – It has been remarkably successful. – I wish them good luck. – It is a healthy, independent enterprise. – Met Uncle Bob, the crazy musician. – He advised above all things to keep away from Shore – and have no further connection with that curst clan.

The diary now moves back to events after those recorded in the previous chapter.

TUES 31 JULY Spent the day at Foxholes Lodge. – A greadley splash o'thunner-rain kept mo i'th'hease till neet'. –
[259] Resolved
    To make list of Debts
    To give notice to quit the house in Gorse St.

To buy Horse Hair Belt
To make epitome of conjugal miseries
and cause of them.

AUG 13TH [*this was a Monday*] – Came away from Lower Shore, my wife carrying the child, and I two bundles of clothes. – Got to Littlebro' just in time to be too late for the train. – A spring cart, laden with empty pop-bottles, was just starting from Littlebro' Wakes to Rochdale. – We got in, and made thither. – got out at the end of Foxholes Lane. – Went to Sally's. – Begun to talk bitterly. – O hell! hell! Without mercy! – Packt up a bed, and bolster which Sally lent us, and sent a porter with them up to the Railway. – Called at my mother's for the rocking chair. – Left by the 7 o'clock train. – I had only six pence left, when we reach [*sic*] Manchester with the luggage, and one of the porters, asked [260] 1/6 for the carriage of the luggage up to Hulme. – I set him off with the things, and Sally with him, and I and Mary Ann, with the child in her arms, set out wondering how I was to raise the other shilling for the man. I stept into Scotts and asked his wife to lend me a shilling. – She gave me the shilling, as if it had been one of her teeth. – we followed Sally and the porter, and found them, gaping about for us in Medlock Street. – They did not know the house. – We entered, made a fire, and the most we could of the little we had, for the night. –

17 AUGUST [*Friday*] – Paid Coupe 8/-, for which he gave me a receipt on behalf of Mrs. Caddy. – O the happiness of paying off an old tormenting debt! – or a debt of any kind. – Bowker asked me to write for a copy of the Rules of the Rochdale Co-operative Store. – Saw a sign over a door in Lower Mosley Street, 'Knocking-up, any hour in the morning.' – Little Dick's marlocks. – His laugh, and crow. – Money expended this week: –––––.

[261] **21 AUG** [*Tuesday*] – Went to Francome's Cirque Nationale in the evening, with Mary Ann. – The Bivouac of Austrelitz [*sic*] – Thought on Napoleon. – Walk by St. John's and Quay St. – Cobden's House.

22 AUG. [*Wednesday*]– Resolving from day to day, to begin my studies in Mathematics and History again, in an orderly and regular manner.
A chat and a smoke in Winstanley's Parlor [*sic*] at Miles Platting. – He took me to see the ground work of the new Baths and

Wash-houses of which he laid the stone a few days ago. – Sir Benj Heywood is the liberal Patron of this, and every institution of a Publicly Beneficial kind, in the neighbourhood.

Dinner not ready again. – Another row. – Every trifle originates domestic wars. – what a damned life! – A world of underground bitterness, and uncongeniality has burnt us ['up' deleted] into tinder, and the slightest spark sets all a-fire. – There is no hotter hell than a discordant fireside.

[262] The idea of <u>Duty</u> – What is the nature of its power over me?

Conversation with Espinasse about John Mills' Sonnet on his Wife's birthday. –

'Beauty's high genesis'

How his little wife is passably pretty enough, but was there ever such stuff as <u>that</u>. – 'I wish there was an Exodus of all <u>such</u> false rigmarole from the world.' – No, no, – Speech was not given to man for such purposes as <u>that</u>, Mr Waugh,' said Espinasse. – Esp. – recommended Cowper's translation of Homer to me, – which he was reading. –

31 AUGUST [*Friday*] – A pipe with Old Jem Wheatherley at the Blue Bell. – Maudlin extravaganzas of drunken fools!

SUN. 2 SEPTR. – Terribly-grand thunder-storm in the night! – I looked out into the yard. – I saw the vivid lightning flash ['*and fall*' *inserted*] like silver – rain in the deep darkness of the night. – The rain came down long and very-heavily. – The streets were rivered. I never heard anything so sublime as [263] the sound of that storm in the silence of night. – Melancholy fits. – Walk in the Evening. – The bright full moon. –

'Meek nature's evening comments are the framing shows and vanities of man.' –

Reading 'Sartor Resartus'. – Thoughts on writing the journal of my own life. – Incidents. – Epochs [?] – companions – Occupations. –

Collected remainders of the Edu. Reg. and squared accounts with the Booksellers. –

MONDAY, 3 AUG. [*September!*] – Cadging cunningry [*sic*]. – Begging philisopily [*sic*]. Jos. Brothertons. – Discussion with Bowker about Deity. – He is one of Robert Owen's fact-worshipping fry. –

FRIDAY, 7 AUG. [*September*] – Went to the County Court, just in time to pay Staveley, before the case was brought on. – Another devil laid, thank heaven! Cameron and Espinasse. – Cameron put to his shifts. The ladies' Anti-Slavery Meeting at the Office. – 'Mind you <u>make</u> no slaves, ladies.' – My mind and heart's sad unravelment. – life and air! – 'Existence is itself so great a fact, that the manner of it matters little.' – Let it be Hearth stone discourse! [264] Household discords again. – The damndest of all damnations! What does it mean? Is there a Plan in it? If so, what? – Go on, and think. – Mary Ann's old Aunt came to-day. – I would sooner see the devil, than any of her race. – The poor little lad! – What is there waiting for him? Query. O – Books. – Letters to write. – Emerson's [?] study.

> The man lost in the details of life
> The man who is master of them.
> View of the Universe, Man, and his life.

SUNDAY 9TH AUG. [*September*] [*More retrospection then:*]
Resolved, again
To eat no more than 2 meals a day next week
To rise at Seven every morning next week.
[265] Still reading that singular book '<u>Sartor</u> <u>Resartus</u>' or 'The Tailor Patched'. – A noble book! Amid all that wild, strong, elevated hurly burly, some passages of wonderful delicacy and pathos! – sauntered about the gardens in the neighbourhood of Ruby St with the little lad in my arms. – Wrote to John Stephens. –

Mathematical calculations fill up the rest of the page.

[266] **MONDAY, 10TH SEPTR.** – Canvassed for Subscriptions. – Espinasse and I had a long conversation respecting the commencement of a fortnightly periodical, to be called 'The Inspector'. – To be entirely devoted to original articles upon the chief political ['*and social*' *inserted*] questions of the day, and literary criticisms. – To be the size of the Athenaeum except that it is to consist of only eight pages. – Price 2d. – The whole editorial control and proprietorship to be vested in Espinasse. Little 'Mirabeau'[6] offers to find the requisite cash, and lend it to little 'Diogenes' unconditionally. – The time seems favorable [*sic*]

---

[6] This is John Stores-Smith. See note in People and Places.

to such an enterprise in Manchester. – The Short-time advocates, whose cause Espinasse and his friends in this matter warmly espouse, are lost for the want of men of talent to aid them and lead them. – Espinasse's style, altho' evidently Carlyle-ridden, has still much that is originally felicitous and striking in it. – There will be little risk in the matter, and he can pull up any time without being too deeply implicated. – Then there will be the sweetness of independence about it which is no [*word missing*].

Pages 267 and 268 are taken up with formal reflections on the difference between 'the gentleman's hall and the poor man's cottage' and the nature of happiness.

[269] **TUESDAY, 11TH SEPTR.** – *[More exclamations of unhappiness and a standard English poem of lost love fill this page.]*

[270] Committee Meeting in the evening. – Glass of Ale and a smoke with Esp. at the Blue Bell in Strangeways. – It is an excellent Inn, and well frequented by what is called 'the best company.' – I have often been amused by a way that Espinasse has of exhibiting his damned Scotch generosity, that makes the folk wonder what he means. – He has a way, when the waiter brings back his change, of flinging down a penny on the table, with a ludicrous, patronising air, and saying, 'See, there's a penny for you.' – The dandy-waiter, who, I'll be bound, has more money of his own than Esp. ever had, or will have, – hesitates, stares at the little queer-looking, spectacled creature an instant, then, seeming to comprehend it, he looks round the room at the ill-concealed mirth of the company, picks up the penny and with an air of mock-gratitude, thanks the donor, turns on his heel with a wink on his eye, and, heaving the penny from one hand to the other, he disappears in the bar, where the mistress, her daughters and maids are, and from whence in a short time, a smothered titter breaks out. – I have often wondered that he cannot see it. – It is altogether a treat to me to see the little air of munificence with which he bestows his penny, and the astonishment and comic thankfulness of the receivers. – [271] We two are as well-known now as any that go there. – They look and whisper, and grin at us between the ale-pumps in the bar as we go in and out.

Conversations about the 'Inspector' – project. – Estimates for printing. – Fittest printer and publisher. – Subscribers. – Price. –

Credit. – Advertising. – Chances of general Sale in Manch. – Sale in neighbouring towns. – Friendly hands that would push it. – Estimate of general expence [sic]. Literary aid to depend on. – It seems to me, every-thing considered, a feasible enterprise, with this exception, that Espinasse is fitful in business of any sort, – and unpersevering, – and from this cause, I prophesy, it will go down, – if somebody else do not catch it in the fall, and sustain it. – but time will tell. – I will do all I can for him and it. –

WEDNESDAY, 12TH SEP. – Staid at home till Noon. – Canvassed for Subscriptions. – Read Cary's Memoir of Chadderton [sic], the Poet.

> 'The marvellous boy,
> The sleepless soul that perished in its pride.'

[272]

> Noo aw gu up un deawn
> This soot ozl't teawn,
> Aw see it's weel stock't wi' preychin plazes;
> But six days I'th' week
> From morning to neet
> Thur moastly shut up I'foke's fazes.
> Nu aw say to mysel,
> Thir wickwi o'deol
> Nur thirn ut ale heases ub th' cayrus.

> I' th' seven, one day
> Th' parsons ul pray,
> Un rant un roar obeawt salvation;
> But th' tother six
> Ur o'owd Nicks
> He may lap his tale reound th' congregation.
> Whol th' parson taks
> His natural snacks
> O' meight, drink, sleep, un ray-cray –ashun,
> He'll have his heaven
> Six days i'th'seven,
> One's quite oneuch to feyght damnation

[273] *A page of mathematical calculations and an unattributed quotation.*

[274] *A short quotation on city life from Sartor Resartus fills half a page. The rest of the page is blank.*

[275] **TUESDAY 25TH SEPTR, 1849.** – Took a walk with Espinasse after the Committee Meeting. – An hour with him at the Blue Bell. – Conversations respecting Sophocles' Antigone, Byron's Werner [*sic*], Macbeth etc. etc. – Shakspere [*sic*] the only poet who has embodied the struggle between destiny and free-will.

WEDNESDAY, 26TH. Meeting of the Organization Committee in the Evening. About 30 of the most respectable and intelligent of the Working Men of Manchester present. – Conversation respecting the best means of widely-interesting the Working classes in this plan of General education. Proposition to address the different Trade Unions upon the subject. – The distribution of printed information. Extensive canvassing. Lectures. – Public Meetings.

At the close of the meeting I went to the clerk at St. Jude's to get tickets for myself and my wife to go by the cheap trip to Blackpool in the morning at 6 o'clock.

THURSDAY 27TH. Rose at 5 o'clock and washed myself all over in cold water. My wife not ready and not disposed to be. I determined that I would not this time (as I have done before so often) let her incurable tardiness keep me at home too, ill-tempered and disappointed. – She was saucy, and I was vexed at her unreasonableness and her shiftlessness. Off I went. The morning was beautifully clear and the air bracing. – There is something touching in the still appearance of a great city at such an hour. When I got into Medlock Street, a woman stood with one of the morning coffee stalls which are out at that time in different quarters of the city. – I took a cup with her, for which she charged me a half penny. – She had no bread and butter, which I much regretted. – But, on [276] I went, and found a larger stall on Medlock Bridge, surrounded by a lot of hungry Mechanics regaling themselves with Coffee and Bread and Butter and Currant Cakes, of which there was no stint on the table. However, the woman had not been overpowered with business before I went, for she hadn't change for a shilling.

I got a satisfactory breakfast with her, and had some jocular conversation with the workmen about, and then went on my way towards the Salford Station. I went down Deansgate, and when I got into the neighbourhood of St. John's, (where I was struck by the spaciousness of the streets, and the number of fine old houses there, for the most part empty. – Cobden's house among the number) I saw large parties of people, seemingly of all conditions of life, but chiefly working folk, and, for the most part women in their holiday dress, walking gleefully in the same direction and talking of the fineness of the morning, the provisions they had in their baskets, bottles etc., and the bachelors, with sweethearts. All this added to my delight, and I felt as if all the world was one house, and all the men and women in it near and dear relations – When I got to the ['station' omitted] [277] a few minutes before six, I found an astounding gathering of people. – The cackle of human voices was stunning, about their dresses, and their tickets, and their companions, and the train. – Upwards of 2000 persons there – all "fudgin fain" and very troublesome cattle to keep out of harm's way, so restlessly resolved were they to rush up and down, from one side of the station to the other, and explore every nook of the buildings, and get into everything in the shape of a railway carriage, in spite of the efforts of the guards and the porters to keep them in bounds till the train was ready. – After much impatient waiting, and speculation as to how soon the train would be ready to get into and start, a long line of carriages pushed slowly into view about 200 yards up the line, and stopt there, evidently with the intent of moderating the eager competition for seats which takes place among such crowds of pleasure-hunters as these. – No sooner were they seen, however, than nearly the whole of them set off at a devil-take-the-hindmost canter towards the carriages, screaming and laughing, and rivin' and tearin' to get into them, as if the whole of the round world was giving way elsewhere. – However, I felt more amused to see it, than to be in it, and knowing there would be room found for us all, I waited till the main rush was over, and then got quietly put by one of the guards into a carriage that wanted one of the due number of passengers. I had the fortune to light among a pleasant company. [278] All women, but an old tee-total reed-maker who sat opposite to me, and a modest looking young man, seemingly of the clerk species, altho' by the way modesty is anything but a characteristic of the Manchester Clerk. One of the women had a lively-looking little child, which was handed round to be nursed and kist by everybody in the carriage. I have noticed how wonderfully little children wake up the heavenliest part of every heart they come near. The coarsest most world-soiled nature meeting with these little, innocent, unconscious crowers, seems softened and shamed into gentleness. These angelic little men! Heaven have them all in its keeping and touch the hearts of all men and women to a wise and delicate care for their culture. At last we began to cleave the bracing air of the morn, and every heart seemed to thrill with exhilaration. The country between Manchester and Preston was remarkably picturesque. We had a fine view of Rivington Pike and the hills in that neighbourhood. At "Proud Preston" we halted a quarter of an hour while the horse drank. Everyone that wished got out here, and walked about the line, within certain bounds, kept by policemen. Off we went gain, and the country became leveller, and exclusively agricultural, and – judging by mine own – very agreeably relieving to Manchester wearied eyes and spirits There is something so manly and sweetly natural about agricul[279]tural occupations that, I believe the generality of men have an inclining to it, and especially the slavers at the sedentary town crafts contemplate country life and labors with a yearning delight. To me the green solitudes, ['and' crossed out] the ['whole' inserted] fair face of nature is a medicinal 'joy for ever' – none but they who, loving nature passionately have been long, perforce, immured in the fume of some large city can perfectly understand the inevitable purifying delight awakened in the heart by such a visit to the country as we had that lovely morning. As we went on towards "the Fylde country" the substantial farmsteads were farther between – the farms evidently larger, and more grain grown upon them. The crops were nearly all in, and large numbers of fine young cattle and sheep roamed about the pastures, and large flocks of geese were in the stubble-fields, gleaning the scattered grain. At Poulton-le-Fylde we stopt till the regular morning train from Blackpool had come down thence, as there is only one pair of rails from Poulton down to Blackpool. – In a few minutes it came, and we went on to the finish of our pleasant journey.

The train was such an uncommon length that, when we stopt, we, who sat in the latter carriages, were some distance from the station. I got out, and seeing the weary delay and difficulty there would be in wriggling one's self through such [280] a mass of people, and being eager, too, to get to the sea, I ran up the slope from the Station Platform and climbed over the rails at the top. The pent-up dense crowd of stragglers below reminded me of the passage of the children of Israel through the Red Sea. Down towards the town I ran, where I immediately remarked the extremely neat, and clean look of the houses, and then I looked down the main street which ran straight down to the glorious green sea. which seemed to stand up at the end of it like a wall of foaming billows. – I went towards it delighted, and blind to everything else for the time. – Down the pebble-paved slope, on to the beautiful beach, which is remarkably expansive, and favorable [sic] to sea-bathing here. In a few minutes the whole of the immense crowd of human cattle which three hours before was in Manchester, was sporting about on Blackpool Sands, like midges in the sunbeam. Every-body seemed to understand that the time of stay in this novel and beautiful region was limited and, therefore went to work instantly to suck all the pleasure they could out of it, – after the Manchester fashion, ['work while you work, play while you play' inserted]. There was a great [word missing] of rough, gaunt-looking ponies there, and of the stupidest, comicalest jack-asses that ever walked the earth since the days of Balaam. – Nevertheless, every four-footed creature on the sands, was, in a twinkling, bestridden by [deletion] one of the children of Adam, and urged to its mettle, – where it happened to have any. [281] And the fun that arose therefrom was infinite. – For some of the asses had an acquired trick of lying down with its rider upon the sand, when it had got a little distance from the starting place, and the rider, lord or lady, rolled over, to the great amusement of the crowd. Some wouldn't stir at all; some would do nothing but kick; but the best of them wouldn't stir an inch past a certain spot on the sands, where, to our eyes, there was no visible boundary mark, but the donkies [sic], one and all, turned round there of their own accord, and made the best of their way home again to the jack-ass stand. Some wags got up mimic tilting-matches, and, with abundance of difficulty and merriment, un-jackassed one another the best way they could. All was glee, wherever I lookt – Some looking about the beach for shells and stones, some sitting in merry groups upon the slope, regaling themselves with the contents of their baskets. Some lounging about with a quiet, contemplative joy beaming in their countenances. Some all boisterous hilarity and limb-frolic. Here they were rushing in and out of the bathing-vans and splashing about in the water like a congregation of mermen and mermaids. There they were hotly competing for admission into a boat which was carrying passengers to a small vessel with two masts, which stood further out in the water. – I bathed once before dinner, and had a ride upon Sancho's Dapple and went out in the sailing vessel on a trip which [282] took more than an hour. – There were two glee singers on board, who sung "O'er the green sea" and other such songs. – I was listening with delight to the lashing of the water against the vessel's side. – On coming ashore again from the trip, I felt hungry, and walked up into the town to cast about for a feed. I looked at the hotels, but their appearance sorted ill with the state of my pocket, so I walked on to look for some accommodation of a genuine character, with humbler pretensions. Coming to a little grocer's shop, I went in to buy a few biscuits, and enquired where I should be able to get a comfortable dinner without going to hotel-expenses. – I could have dined heartily and satisfactoryily [sic] enough with a lump of cheese and some apples, in the open air, but mine was an extraordinary hunger that day, and my heart was bent on a cosy chat in a chimney nook, and a hearty feed on "summat at deed by a knife". The flesh pots of Egypt were rolling up and down my thoughts, and I could not endure vegetarian diet on such a day as that was – The good mistress of the shop said they sometimes cookt meat for visitors, who went out and purchased according to their liking; and that she would be glad to do so for me, if I chose, and, as it was just their own dinner-time, she could accommodate me comfortably with all the vegetable trimmings to a good dinner. [283] I was fain to hear it, and bolted off to the Shambles, which I found after many enquiries, and bought a pound of good mutton chops, which I wrapt up in a paper, and hurried back with to the good wife who had undertaken the cooking of them. – In a quarter of an hour all was ready for me, – I had been ready some time, and fell to with a good will. – Espinasse says to me sometimes that I am in many things the counterpart of Cervantes' Sancho. – If he had been behind me that day, upon the asses, and at meals, he would have sworn that I was the same man. – I finished my meal, and the good wife charged me fourpence for the trouble of cooking my chops, and for the trimmings to them, which I handed to her with "mony braw thanks", and took my way slowly to the seaside again. On my way thither, however, I stept into the Beach Hotel, to get a glass of porter. The lobby was adorned with marine plants, shells and other sea-treasures. I was shown into a well-furnished and ornamented room called "The Tap", where half-a-dozen men in the garb of gentlemen sat joking together, and regaling themselves with whiskey. One of them particularly 'took my eye'. – He a pedantic old fellow in spectacles, with a very supercilious look, who set himself up ['*evidently*' *inserted*] as the wit and scholar of the party. – as to his learning he wore what rags of it he had upon his tongue's end, in the shape of old moth-eaten Latin ['*School*' *inserted*] Delectus phrases, and his wit was a pitiful kind of punning [284] or word-juggling to show that he had a mouthful more of the trick work of talk than his more sensible and silent neighbours. But his freaks seemed to me more like the labored antics of an old worn out word-mountebank than the charming grace and world activity of a real wit. I went out and walked down to the beautiful frontier of the kingdom of Neptune. I walked along the surgy fringe of the green sea, with a delighted heart. Then went out in a van, and bathed in the sea again. After that I met with the old tee-totaler [*sic*] who sat opposite to me in the carriage in the morning. We got into a rude kind of chariot, the body of which was not unlike a slice ['*the half*' *deleted*] of a pew in a Methodist chapel, only the wood was of all sorts and thicknesses, and ill-joined, with great shifters between the joinings, and the material looked as if it had been partly orange-boxes, and partly an old pair of drawers. – This primitive vehicle was drawn by ['*by*' *repeated*] a "tit" of rather better than the common sort about here, which are, for the most part, half-starved and ill-groomed, having chiefly, I believe to "fund fer thersels" as we say about Rochdale. In about an hour, we went up together into the town, and walked through the very pretty, and, for this place, large covered Market place, which we found crowded with fruit stalls, books, boots and shoes, baskets; and all kinds of trinketry, which latter are [285] greatly bought up here by the visitors, as presents for those they've left behind 'em. It began to approach the time for the train to start back, and the folk beginning to slowly incline towards the Station, we, too, took the road thitherwards. We were at the spot in good time, and, again I had the fortune to light among an agreeable carriage full of folk. The bathing, the sea air, and the exercise of one sort and another made me feel very comfortable when seated, and rather inclined to fall asleep, but, what with the lively talk of my travelling companions, and the merriment that was going on outside the carriages, I was forced to give it up, and join in. And then, every two or three minutes, the carriage door was clunked open, and a red-faced man, with a piece of printed blanket round his neck, looked in earnestly, and shouted out "Is thur any reawm." – "Eh, neaw," was the constant reply, and after a little wrangling, sometimes, down they poppt one after another – to look for rest elsewhere. Soon as the train was full – "Bubub! Bubbub! Bubbubbub!" off we went homewards just as

> "the rosy rays of evening fell"

and the dreamy robe of twilight began to float over the quiet "Fylde". – The women struck up the "Vesper Bell", and away we sped, the buz [*sic*] of voices in the train gradually sinking lower and lower [286] till, except here and there, where some roystering bottle-sucker kept the carriage in a roar, the talk became mostly a gentle hum to which no inconsiderable number of snores contributed their somnolent share. The sea wind, ['*and*' *deleted*] the ['*length of the*' *added*] journey ['*from early morn*' *deleted*], and the gleeful life of the day, 'from morn to dewy eve,' had sung and rockt numbers of them to a healthy slumber. – The daylight had scarce yet left us when the moon uprose to smile on us and light us to the lovely scenes through which we travelled back. The [*deletion*] kine had been milkt, and gone lowing to their housing. – The cottars had laid their tools by for the day. – here and there at the farm-houses and little dwellings of the rustic poor ['*that stood*' *inserted*] each in its sweet encirclement of green, from the country mansion, and the clustering village, the bed-lights gleamed through the trees in the still night, and the day ['*closed*' *deleted*] shut in with the most beautiful and soothing pictures of tranquility that the eye of man could light upon.

> 'Meek nature's evening comments
> On the fuming shows and vanities of man.'

The train reach [*sic*] Salford at 20 minutes to 10 o'clock, and I was at home in Hulme at 10.

Thus ended this pleasant day.

[287] *A page of Addition, Subtraction and Multiplication.*

[288] **SUNDAY, 30TH SEPTEMBER, 1849.** – Rainy day. – Passed the day at home, – a day of rich quietness! – Writing and reading. – Resolved to commence the writing of extracts from Sartor Resartus tomorrow.

'To morrow, didst thou say?
Methought I heard Horatio say to-morrow.'

MONDAY, 1ST OCTOBER, 1849. – Occupied all day in getting speakers for the public Meeting at Crumpsall on Wednesday, the 3rd, in collecting Subscriptions ['*for the Association*' *inserted*] and in getting a few Subscriptions to the 'Inspector'. – Got David Morris, Dr. Watts, and Thomas Layton, as speakers, got £2. 2. 6 in Subscriptions to the Association; and got eighteen Subscribers to the 'Inspector', five of whom paid in advance. – Longing to see Macready as 'Iago' in Othello. – "Oh, the weary want o'sillar!" – Manchester Eating Houses. – The various character, and characteristics of them. –

The rest of the page is taken up with mathematical calculations.

[289] **TUESDAY, 2ND OCTOBER, 1849.** – Busy all day with the canvassing craft. – Committee Meeting in the evening. Quarrel between Espinasse and Smith Phillips Robinson about the Czar of Russia, and the Hungarian Refugees at the Court of the Big Turk. – Robinson is a conceited bully, altho', in practical, world-knowledge, – a clever man. Espinasse has more knowledge of books than of men, is ['*a*' *inserted*] dreamy, impulsive ['*and sensitive creature – who*' *inserted*] often forgets Carlyle's last word of advice to him when he left him in London – 'avoid furor?' Robinson often treats him with unwise contempt, and butts at him boorishly on account of his ['*seeming*' *inserted*] helplessness in practical matters. Espinasse has something too 'Scotch' in one sense about him for me, but, he is, nevertheless, as honest as steel, and a man of genius and learning, and I have ten times the respect for him that I have for Robinson, who seems to me, a very egotistical, coarse, and blustering Mr Knowall. Cup of tea at Scotts. – Discussion of the Vegetarian Principle. – Animalculae. New scheme of 'Cyphers' to elude Telegraphic exhorbitance ['*expences*' *deleted*]. A simpler system of Phonography than Pitman's. Walked home by the light of the moon, thinking of my wife and child, of means of living and paying my debts, of the bright star of independence for ever beaming before me, of the chances and changes of this mortal existence, of moral purity, stern resolution, and a brave readiness to face the worst that fate can send me. –

[290] *One calculation and then blank.*

[291] **WEDNESDAY, 3ʳᴰ OCTOBER, 1849** – Went with Espinasse and Dr. Watts to the Public Meeting at Crumpsall. – Made a short speech, – very unsatisfactory to myself. – returned together in a coach, at Ten o'clock. – At six o'clock this evening, my wife came to the Office to me with the keys of the house. She said she was going to Rochdale. She was determined to go. – I was astonished, alltho' [*sic*] somewhat used to this sort of business with her. – However she showed a disposition to brawl, and I made little attempt to dissuade her from going, because I knew it would be useless to do so. – But I was something more than grieved about it. – Nothing but disaster, or, at least, a perpetuation of matrimonial misery can result from such proceedings. – I knew not what to do. – and letting her go her way, if she chose; but I knew if I did so, she would find her own opportunity in spite of me. – I should be glad to be freed from her honorably, but, in my circumstances, that is impossible. – If we were to part for ever I should be happier than I am, if I was sure that well would come upon her. – But I am full of anxiety on her account.

[292] **THURSDAY, 4ᵀᴴ OCTOBER, 1849.** – Lay in bed, ill, till past Noon. – Rose, washed, made a fire, got a meal of Milk and Bread. Went down to town. – Staid at the Office till Six o'clock. Went with Johnson to see Macready perform 'Richlieu' [*sic*]. – Sat up late writing. – Wrote to Stephens.

A period intervenes here in the course of which my mind and body were so harassed between debt and the weight of constant anxiety, and sorrow pressing continually on my mind through domestic troubles that my health trembled fearfully in the balance of life and death, and I walked about as silent and pensive as if I was following my own funeral, – which, in truth, we are all doing. –

[293] **1ˢᵗ JANUARY, 1850.** [*Tuesday*] – New Year's Day.

There is a paragraph of sad reflection ending 'Poor Mary Ann!'

I have undertaken the <u>Sub-Editorship</u> of the <u>Inspector</u>.[1] I was busy late last night dispatching the Bookseller's parcels and the copies to the subscribers. The same to-day till 3 a.m. Got <u>The Monastery</u> from the Circulating Library to relieve the sadness of my thoughts a little. [*Further sad reflection follows.*]

Page 294 has further attempts at verse. Page 295 has a short quotation form Carlyle, 296 is blank, 297 is made up of part of general reflections on society, 298 reflections on abstinence, 299 four topic headings, pages 300 to 304 are blank.

[305] **9ᵀᴴ MARCH, 1850.** [*Saturday*] – How many serious causes for thought and care there are about my path just now, – how many for regret, arising out of the past. – But I must and will endeavour to concentrate all powers upon the necessities of the present moment, and, heaven endow me with the wisdom and the strength to lay one stone wright [*sic*] every day, towards the rebuilding of the ruined hopes of my pure childhood. – There is one theme which is continually either a flaming madness or a smouldering sorrow within me, eating up my heart and thoughts, – my wife and child! – What can I do? And then, the precarious state of my poor mother's health. When she dies, what a gap there will be in the world to me! My poor, infirm, hard-wrought, hard-tried mother. – Nothing can make up for the loss of her to me. –

It is striking 12. – I will into bed, and read myself to sleep.

10ᵀᴴ MARCH, 1850. [*Sunday*] – Spent a few hours with Ridings, Stenthal, David Morris, and Horner at Scott's. – Riding read us a poem of no small beauty and a pathos, called 'The Burial of Burns', written by a young native of Bury, of the name of Taylor, an ardent admirer of the famous bard of Scotland, and much imbued with his spirit. – He (Ridings) read it judiciously, and favored [*sic*] by his fine voice, it

---

1   This project with Espinasse had no success.

was very effective, and stirred up my petrifying soul into enthusiastic life for a few moments. – Played a few games at draughts. – Walked home into Hulme. – Stopt to listen to a poor Scots man in the street, singing 'My Nannie, O', in a way that delighted me. I followed him a while en[306]chanted with the song, which has charmed me with the simplicity of the strain, and the purity of love embodied in it, ever since I was a boy. – It needs no learning to teach men that Burns' songs are fine! – They are gems of a fine heart, flowing with humanity. – The whole street felt this simple song, and followed the slow steps of the singer, with intense heed. – Rich and poor, all felt this universal appeal from the heart of a man, to all hearts that might beat after him. –

TUESDAY, 12TH MARCH, 1850. – As I walked down Market Street this afternoon, I heard a shout raised a short distance behind me. I turned, and saw what I thought to be a large black dog wriggling under the wheel of a large wagon, very heavily laden with sacks of flour. When I went nearer, I saw a man's leg playing in the air in an agony of convulsion. One of his thighs was under the wheel, close to the body, and was completely squashed out into a thin cake of bloody smush. – He was uttering a wail so unearthly and horrible that it made me sick. – * * * *. Think of the deadly earnestness of the devotees of Juggernaut.

WEDNESDAY, 13TH MARCH, 1850. – A day of painful doubt and anxiety. – Wrote to John Stephens of Liverpool. – A dreadful head-ache came upon me towards night, and I sauntered to Scott's, and lounged there till 11o'clock. – Gen. Co. Meeting. –

[307] **THURSDAY, 14TH MARCH, 1850.** – Discussions with Scott's Teetotal Advocates. – I have done nothing towards the imperative and urgent task that lies before me. – Went to hear the Rev – Bardsley lecture against our Association's Educational Plan, and against the tendency of the times to give 'undue importance to intellectual culture' was he said in another phrase, – 'to expel God from everything'. – 'Contempt of Religion and the Bible.' – 'The separation of the Religious from the Secular' – these were the points, or rather phantasies of his own creation, against which he fulminated his clerical thunder without stint.

FRIDAY, 15TH MARCH, 1850. – Still wandering in thought, lax of purpose and inferior in deed. – O, Great Source of Excellence, help me to work out the desire I feel to be a noble man in everything. – Went to the District Committee's Tea Party, in Dr Scholefield's School Room, in Every Street, Ancoats. – A working man, – one of the Committee, – read an Essay on the 'Plan', which did him credit. – Smiles and Grimshaw and I, addressed the meeting in short speeches. – Altogether, a pleasant, and a useful evening. – Called at Chorlton Hall, on my way home, and found David Morris and his lady, and old Frazer, the Scotch Singer, there. Had a chat and a smoke, and then walked home in the silent midnight, under a clear, star-spangled sky. – O God of heaven, protect me, and inspire me with a continual love of truth in all things and strength to live accordant with it. – O father, forgive me, and sustain me in my way. –

[308] **SATURDAY, 17TH MARCH, 1850.** [*actually the 16th*] – I have spent too much time at Scott's again today. – I am wasting my precious hours in frivolities and in the company of men I do not admire, and would not copy. – Virulent [?] discussions again. – I have the work of two life-times to do in the half of one, which half stands in jeopardy every hour. – If I live out the full term of an healthy life, I shall have enough to do to correct the errors of the first half of my life. – Took 3 dozen pamphlets up to Duffy for sale. – Got home at half past Ten.

SUNDAY, 18TH, MARCH, 1850. [*the 17th*] – In the middle of the night, I was awakened by a dream which I devoutly believe to have been a warning from heaven. I was so impressed by it that I lay some time sleepless and tossing about in a painful meditation. I got up and walked about my bed room a while. I looked through the window. It was just dawn. A few gauzy scattered clouds stood still on the sky's blue field, slightly tinged with the roseate hues that herald the approaching sun. There was nothing astir in the streets below, nor in the heavens above, as I thought, but I looked at the sky again, and was aware the clouds were stealthily changing their shapes and donning the golden robes of morning to meet the monarch of day. – Listening again, I heard a blithe sparrow here and there twittering to his drowsy mates about the time of day, and the fineness of the morning. – And, in the distance, I could hear some early-rising lover of the fields, knocking his neighbour up to go 'a-yarbing' Withington way. – I wrote down some notes in my book – and resolved to keep my eye more thoughtfully [309] upon every step of my life, at this critical and difficult period and to lose time nor opportunity [*sic*] of placing myself in a manly and honourable position before God and Man. – Resolved to make a list of my debts and assets, or sources of payment, to-day, and to keep my eye continually upon my true condition, painful and degrading as it is, until I am fairly extricated and can draw my breath in peace, and owe no man anything. – Read Wordsworth's Poem on Presentiments.

There follows more reflection and self-recrimination, including all the entry for Monday, 18th March 1850. Page 310 is a poem in standard English. Pages 311 lists debts, including £2 to Castleton Overseers presumably for Mary Ann in the Workhouse, Page 312 lists Inspector Subscriptions not yet paid, including Mrs. Gaskell, 121 Upper Rumford St. Page 313 lists people to whom pamphlets on the Movements of the Times should be distributed.

Page 314 is a printed broadsheet copy of 'Go thou balmy morning air', a poem in standard English by Waugh which is superimposed on a different manuscript poem in standard English. Page 315 is a poem in manuscript 'Poor Mary Gray' by Waugh in standard English.

Page 316 is another printed broadsheet copy "Twas Rosy June' by Waugh in standard English, again superimposed on a different manuscript poem in standard English. The girl in this poem is 'Mary Ann'. The poet waits unavailingly but at last she comes to him:

> Go to your beds
> And hide your head
> Ye starry winkers in the sky
> And, moon, beshroud
> Thee in a cloud!
> Leave night to Mary Ann and I.

[317] **TUESDAY, 19TH MARCH, 1850.** – Wrote to the <u>Examiner</u> and to the <u>Guardian</u> regarding the excavation in Altrincham St, into which Foster fell on Sunday night. The two opposite parties gradually getting into a ferment of eagerness for the fray at the 2 great Educational Meetings, – one at the Free Trade Hall on the 28th of March, and the other in the Town Hall, to be presided over by the Mayor, on the 1st of April. – The Executive Meeting brisker than usual tonight. – Spent an hour at Scott's. –

[The entries for Wednesday, 20th March, 1850 and Thursday 21st. March, 1850 which goes over onto page 318 are again full of melancholy introspection ...]

when I go into company, I am apt to rush into the other extreme, and become to appearance, recklessly frivolous, – but there is a strain of bitter desperation under it all, that nobody sees or feels but me ... God help me, I am sometimes as wise as fifty Solomons for a few minutes in speech or writing, but in hard active trial there are few greater fools than me between here and Pendle Hill.

[318] **SATURDAY, 23RD MARCH, 1850.** – Went with David Morris and his wife, and Scott, and Jones, and Grimshaw, the advocater, to see the 'Jewess' performed at the Theatre Royal. – I had previously spent the whole of the afternoon in hot discussion with Elijah Dixon, the defender of William Penn, the Quaker. – The subject of debate was our Association's Plan of Popular Education, and I had the [*continued on page 321*] best of it.

Page 319 contains a crossed out poem in standard English addressed to a 'little maid', Harriet Foster. Page 320 is blank.

[321] **SUNDAY, 24TH MARCH, 1850.** – After dinner, I went down to Shudehill, and took the omnibus to Middleton, or rather, the omnibus took me, – or the horses took us both. I hate to talk or write by the card. But I have seen so much of the ignorant, carpy criticism which prevails among the Temperance Advocates who frequent Scott's Hotel, that the remembrance of their shallow-brained, frosty-hearted fastidiousness came over me just then. The day was very fine, clear, and frosty, and I had a glorious ride. From Middleton I walked up towards Rochdale, but a train coming up when I got to Blue Pits, I went on with it to the end of the journey. – I was glad to find my mother a little relieved from her pain; but she was still very weak. She is evidently sinking fast. Who shall I have left in the world when she is gone, if I live after her? – I called at my sister Ann's, and got my tea there. After that I went up to Foxholes Lodge, and stayed awhile with Sally, who took us through the conservatory, and gave me a few beautiful flowers. – The family was not at home, so I roamed about the lawns and woods, delighted with the scene. – I then went down to the Store News Room, in Toad lane, where I found a party of working men discussing the 'Organisation of Labour' question. I said a few words on the subject, before they broke up; afterwards, I went to see one of the Short Time Committee at the Coach and Horses; thence to my mother's again; and, lastly back to Foxholes Lodge, where I supt and slept. –

[322] **MONDAY, 25TH MARCH, 1850.** – Half past 10 train to Manchester. – Met Miss Irvine at the Station. – Went down to Manchester together. – Preparation for the great meetings coming on. –

TUESDAY, 26TH MARCH, 1850. – Still full of business belonging to the approaching contest. – Rousing the town in all directions. – I am quite an adept at agitation policy now, but at no other kind of useful policy that I know of. – But, if I live, it shall not always be so.

WEDNESDAY, 27TH MARCH, 1850. Busy all day in despatching messengers in all directions with notes, bills, tickets, etc. connected with the Town Hall and Free Trade Hall meetings. The Rev. Hugh Stowell is trying to circumvent us by pre occupying the Town Hall. – He is sending round a paper to be signed by the Church party, pledging themselves to be at the front of the Town Hall in King Street at ½ past Eight in the morning of Monday. – This has become known to our party, and they are resolved to be there before them in sufficient numbers to fill the Hall. The town is hot on both sides of the dispute, but the ['working' inserted] people are all with us most heartily. – We have besides, a large amount of the ['foremost' inserted] intellect and monied influence of Manchester with us, together with clergymen of high repute, of every denomination, from Catholics and Churchmen down to Ranters. Of catholics [sic], we have few openly declared in our favour, but we have at least 3 Catholic priests on the Committee. – In addition to this, just at [323] this crisis, the Catholics of Manchester are unusually embittered against the church party, and their champion Stowell, in particularly [sic], in consequence of the late violent controversies between these two bodies of theologists, which were carried on in a manner which did no honour to either, but which, I believe, on the part of the Episcopalians, was most ungenerous and dishonourable. – The Rev. Father Heron, too, a Catholic priest, highly beloved by the Catholics of Manchester, has not long ago won a trial against Hugh Stowell, for gross defamation of character, with £500 damages. For these reasons, the Catholics are likely to come down to the fray from their dingy dens in George's Road, Little Ireland, Shudehill, Angel Meadows, and Salford, like one man, more perhaps, upon the whole, because they mortally ['hate' inserted] Stowell and the Churchmen, than because they have any enthusiastic love for us.

But, whatever be the nature of the arguments used, I hope those who are in the wrong may go away with a most convincing thrashing. – God speed the right. – This important question is immensely increasing in interest to the popular mind. It is one destined to have immense influence in shaping the future of England. – I am disgusted with many of the fanatic hounds that raise such an ignorant clamour about the separation of the secular from the religious. – 'Let there be light.' True religion has nothing to fear from it. – I had a Meeting of the Officers of the District Committees at eight o'clock. – Supt at Scott's, and walked home in the moonlight with Thompson and Stanley.

[324] **THURSDAY, 25TH MARCH, 1850.** – The day crowded with preparations for the night. – Executive Committee met in the evening. – Fine comfortably-filled meeting at the Free Trade Hall. – The late Mayor of Leicester (Biggs), George Dawson, Peter Rylands, Dr Davidson, Geo. Wilson, Dr Watts, Alex. Henry, M.P. and Jas. Kershaw M.P. were there together with McKerrow, 'Mirabeau',[2] and a host of the elite of Lancashire. – Triumphant result! So far as can be judged by such immense gatherings of the middle, but mostly working classes as these.

Page 325 is taken up with a poem in standard English 'On the death of an unfortunate Friend'. Page 326 is blank. Page 327 has a heavily corrected poem in standard English 'To the Roach' (the river, not the fish). Page 328 is blank.

[329] **MONDAY, 1ST APRIL, 1850.** – Rose at ½ past Seven, washed, breakfasted, and walked down to old Thomas Taylor's, the venerable mechanic, whose name I put upon the list of [*'working men of'* inserted] the deputation from the Free Trade Hall Meeting to the Town Hall Meeting. – He expressed some fears lest his employers (Sharp, Roberts) – who had been always kind to him, and even now, at his advanced age, and nearly blind, still employed him and paid him well, though he was of much less service to them than he was wont to be; – he was afraid lest they should hear of his intermeddling in this affair, and if so, take it so much amiss as to throw him out of employment in his helpless age. I felt for the old fellow, though I could not but feel indignant at something wrong in the present state of social arrangements, in which

---

[2] John Stores-Smith. See note in People and Places.

the man whose only property is his labour can so seldom find a market for as much honest effort of one sort or another as will keep him alive, unless he keep his political opinions chained up in his throttle. – And after spending a precious life-time in the service of another, that he should have such a cause for troubling as this. – However, we walked down Oxford Road together, and put the thing on a safe footing. – The centre of the town astir towards the Town Hall! – The front of the Hall occupied by a crowd of Stowell's party as early as Eight o'clock. – Busy in the office, disposing of such Platform Tickets as had been returned by the gentlemen to whom they had [330] been allotted, and who could not make use of them.

Page 330 is overwritten at right angles in such a way as to make it very difficult to decipher. It deals with details of the meeting.

[331] **3ʀᴅ APRIL, 1850.** – I will use neither tobacco nor snuff today, nor go to Scott's. – Read Carlyle's 'Downing Street'. – Powerful and solemn. – The day busied with Petition preparations, and preparations for Memorial to be presented by our Executive Committee to Lord John Russell, the prime Minister, at the Town Hall, to-morrow noon. –

I have succeeded in getting over one day [*'almost' inserted*] without tobacco, [*'and entirely without snuff' inserted*]! – I will try again tomorrow. – Printer's Bill for my pamphlet came in to-day. How in heaven's name am I to meet the inevitable demands upon me. Courage! Be steady and strive for the best, with a heart prepared for the worst.

4ᴛʜ APRIL, 1850. – I have got over another day without smoking or snuffing, and I will continue to follow the same path. I feel much better for this short abstinence. – Bought a little book by Eardley Wilmott, Barrister, called 'A Few Facts concerning Water' – Fussing about after the Memorial and the Prime Minister! – His Lordship is a man of the clever little species, – a shrewd-looking, dapper fellow, – only that care has been and is carving his face with her quaint devices. – He does not look to me like a man with large sympathies, and a bold genius. – Walking side by side with Potter, our big, good-tempered, greasy-faced, swag-bellied Mayor, they looked like a great stallion with a little pony trotting by its side to set it off. – In answer to an application made to his lordship in the course of the day to receive a deputation from our Committee, with a Memorial praying him to exert his influence for the establishment of a system of Education based upon the principles of the Association's Plan, to which he is known to be favorable [*sic*], – he wrote saying that the necessity for his de[332]parture from Manchester early the following morning prevented him from receiving a deputation, which prevention he regretted, – but desiring that the Memorial might be forwarded to him under cover; – which was done, after running from one end of Manchester to the other [*'till near midnight' inserted*] for the signatures of the Executive Committee to it. – Some of the Committee met in the evening, and a Monster Petition to Parliament from Manchester was agreed upon. – Late to bed again. –

FRIDAY, 5TH APRIL, 1850. – Very late riser this morning. – it looks skulkish and neglectful going to business late. – I wish I had a little more clock-work in my head. – But I will never rest till I am a better man every way than I am now. – Sent Petition Sheets out for signature, and several large packets of Pamphlets [*'of Pamphlets' repeated*] to enquirers for information. – Wrote to Richard Gardner (late M.P. for Leicester). – In the evening I met Elijah Dixon, my old theological Radical friend, with whom I had another hot discussion on the secular and the religious for some three mortal hours. In the course of our talk, – which he carried on with the bible in one fist, and the other clenched to thump the table with, – he introduced such a medley of fag-ends of opinions jumbled together, and thrown out in conglomerate lumps, interlarded with a multitude of scriptural phrases, the pertinent bearing of which I could not for the dull soul of me see, – that I am afraid we both of us bellowed to little purpose, except as far as our internal wind-machinery thereby got some valuable exercise. – But he is a sterling old humbug hater! A most estimable man! Once a poor, hard-wrought factory-lad, – according to [333] his own account, uncommonly shy, and shame-faced, down-hearted, and dissatisfied with his condition in mind and heart, and worldly position, and ever retiring into unfrequented corners to pray to God 'to make him over again,' in the simple earnestness of a child. – After this he took to reading the Bible, where he found comfort and guidance. – And I never met with a man who has that book so completely at his finger-ends as we say. – He has no sired [?] sham-sanctity in his manners, – he is hearty and can laugh vigorously, without being either unbecoming or frivolous. He can talk with thundering earnestness on any topic which interests him, – and his language is thick with scripture. He is now an hale, and, in every sense, an independent old man, in the full possession of all his faculties. – He was a personal friend of William Cobbett's. – From his youth up he has been a man of great note and influence among the Lancashire Radicals. – I feel great respect both for his understanding on most practical matters, and for his moral qualities. – No snuffing, no smoking to-morrow.

SATURDAY, 6TH APRIL, 1850. – Spent the evening at Scott's. Wrangling with Dixon and the Teetotal advocates. – Elijah Ridings was there trying to sell Whittaker's Manchester, and Aiken's History of Lancashire and Cheshire by commission, to raise the wind. – Poor devil! – He had just concluded a bargain with David Morris, and drawn the money, when I happened to turn over the leaves of the History of Lancashire, and found 16 pages out. – It happened to be at an interesting point to me, the history of the custom of 'Riding the Black [334] Lad' in Ashton, and I bawled out without thinking, 'hallo, this book's imperfect.' – this being found so, the bargain was annulled, and the unfortunate poet had to return the money, and [*deletion*]

'gae some where else to seek his dinner.'

And his family's too, with a downcast heart. – I was sorry for him, and wished I had never seen the book. – But I am sure it will turn out the best for him in the long run, for Morris will continue to be a good customer to him in future, whereas, if he had taken the book home, and then found it imperfect, he might possibly have imagined that Ridings fore-knew that the book was not complete, – which I am confident the poor fellow did not know, – and have broken off all traffic with him hereafter, which would have been no small loss to the silver-haired old rhymer. – David Morris and I strolled in a drizzly shower through Knott Mill Fair. – It was just at its height, and the crowd was immense. – Giants, dwarfs, conjurers, gamblers, waxwork figures, travelling theatres, mountebanks, menageries, musicians, cart-auctioneers, glass-workers, automatons, wild Indians, learned pigs, horses that fire guns, nut and gingerbread stalls by the 100, tripe barrows, toffy-merchants with the 'posy' 'I love you' running through their sticks of sweet ware, puff and dart tables, and wheels of fortune, here and there an old book merchant, a tin-stall, and a wooden bread and cheese shop, thimble-[335]riggers keeping a sharp look out for the 'peelers', orange girls, fiddlers, fuddlers, squallers, brawlers, sprawlers, whores, soldiers, beggars, country lads and their sweethearts, dancing rooms with the windows up, and a clatter of music and feet inside, – blue and red lights glowing from the shows, gongs sounding, cymbals clashing, bands playing, pandeau pipes, and barrell organs, speaking trumpets, clowns giving solos on penny whistles, swinging boxes, wooden horses ['*drivers shouting 'Who rides? and' inserted*] Eccles cake vendors crying out 'Tail again,' – women screaming about their toes, their bonnetts [*sic*], and umbrellas, and ['*young' inserted*] men swearing, shouting, elbowing, and rushing to and fro thro' the crowd like young bulls just loosened into a pasture, and lads frolicing [*sic*] here and there switching penny canes about with a brass nail in the head for an ornament, – little children in their mother's arms with basket-rattle in their hands, – but I must stop and take wind. – – –

SUNDAY, 7TH APRIL, 1850. – I have been in an 'hankering swither' all day whether I should go to Rochdale, or not. – I am still full of anxiety and pain of mind on Mary Ann's account, but I see more and more the necessity of avoiding her vicinity. – It is an absolute necessity, if am [*sic*] to do anything hereafter, worthy of a man. – [*deletion*]. I can do no better thing than to avoid her and hers, and the circumstances with scrupulous care, however painful it may be, and I feel a growing indignation at the manner I have been treated. [*Deletion*] The only <u>wise</u> impulse that moved me towards Rochdale to-day was my mother, old, infirm, and in [336] a dangerous state of health.

Page 336 is also overwritten at right angles in a way which makes it very difficult to decipher. He did not go to Rochdale. It includes an entry for Monday the 8th and Tuesday the 9th of April.

[337] **11TH. APRIL, 1850.** Resolved to abstain from smoking to-day. – Canvassed for signatures during the day.

12TH APRIL Take pamphlets to printers
        Get a/c from Owen
        Get No 1 of Inspector
        Get Pamphlets that are needed from Bowker
        Neither smoke ['*at all' inserted*], nor eat at all after six o'clock.
        Send Pamphlets to Bohanna and Bill to Ardrey
        Get returns from Duffy
  – It is now night and I have not smoked to-day, but what other of

the above resolutions have I fulfilled?

I have sold about 70 Pamphlets, at an 'Alarming Sacrifice', but I want to [*deletion*] turn them into money, and I cannot wait.

> I will endeavour once again
> To break my sensual slavery,
> Nor ever yield till I attain
> A life of truth and bravery.
>
> Whatever hurts soul or body's health
> [*deletions*]
> My dearest joys congealing
> I'll shun like hell; – my highest wealth
> Shall be true thought and feeling.

Went to Rochdale on the **13TH** [*Saturday*] and saw my mother, whom I was happy to find much better in health and spirits. Another respite from the inevitable doom, and from my sad bereavement. I never hear one of those solemn old Methodist tunes which the country folk in the hills and dales of Blackstone Edge are so fond of, but my poor mother and my childhood rushes in a stream through my heart! – In the immortality of the soul, alone, can I find any satisfaction for the sorrow of my mother's life, and for my loss of her in this world. – I saw my wife's aunt in [338] Rochdale and it woke up the smouldering misery of my heart into a flame that will be ['*many many*' inserted] days and sleepless nights before it slackens again. – My poor wife and child. Heaven, in its justice hath chosen thus to punish the errors of my youth, and in this thought, alone, can I find resignation and strength to pursue my path with determination to live purely and nobly the remainder of my days. May he who governs and sees all aid me to overcome my evil passions, and to grow every moment a better man in thought and deed.

I have had many hot discussions at Scott's these few days with different persons of the opposite party, on the Secular Education plan. – our great Petition for the Commons on the subject was got up during last week, and I dispatched it on Tuesday evening, the 16th to the right Honorable [*sic*] T. Milner Gibson M.P. for presentation.

On Monday night, **15TH**, the Church party held a meeting in the Corn Exchange, for the inauguration of an Address to Mr. Hugh Stowell, complimenting him, – in language that to me sounded fulsome, – on 'the piety of spirit,' and the ' Christian deportment' which has [*sic*] exhibited in his late brave advocacy of Scriptural Education. The admission to the meeting was the same as to all the previous meetings of that party on this question, since the beginning of the controversy, – by tickets, carefully distributed as far as possible, to their own party, and pledging every one ' not to disturb nor interrupt the proceedings.' – and yet the address purported to be from 'the Working Men of Manchester.' Had it been from his own admirers alone, nobody could have objected to it; but 'the Working Men of Manchester' means something more than that inconsiderable body 'the Operative Conservative Association.' However, some persons who did not agree with the sentiments of that address, and could not tamely listen to the blackguard aspersions launched against the Secular Education party by the unscrupulous serfs who were put forth as the orators of that evening, did get in, and attempted to express their dissent from the proceedings, but they were, according to prepared arrangements, forcibly ejected by the police. – The meeting was a very rough one. – [339] But the meeting at the Free Trade Hall, on the following evening, for the presentation of the Address to the meek-spirited Canon of Chester, was an unparalleled scene in the history of this public dispute. Some person or persons, unknown, 'neither fearing God nor regarding man' – having neither sense of justice nor even of worldly policy in them, had got some thousands of forged tickets printed, and distributed among the working men of the town, who came down with them in immense numbers. It was an ill advised act in every sense, whether it was well-intended to us or not. However, the forgery was discovered before the doors were opened, and every person who held one of those spurious tickets was turned back. The crowd outside was double that inside, and rampant with indignation. But that the head of the police repulsed them, they would have broken into the Hall. The streets were crowded and the people outside were addressed by Dr Watts from a cart, in St. Peter's Square, near the scene of the famous 'Peterloo massacre.' Other speakers addressed the crowd in knots, in different parts of the neighbourhood. Watts got a Petition to Parliament passed unanimously by his auditors, and he dispatched it to Parliament the same night, with a letter explaining the circumstances of the whole affair. – I was admitted by a private door to the 'League Box' into which our Committee came shortly after. We had a full view of the whole affair inside. – In the disgraceful speech of that evening, Stowell completely out-Stowelled himself. The virulence

and ignorance he displayed were really amazing. Let the papers that report the transactions of that night speak of this. The police had ample employment in putting out those who uttered any impression of dissent from his blackguard thunder. – At the close, the crowd outside rushed in such a body about his carriage that the police had to charge against them in line, and to protect the carriage, with its precious load of ecclesiastical humbug, down the street.

[340] **FRIDAY, 19TH APRIL, 1850.** – I have just returned from spending the evening with Simms, the author of 'Hours of Solitude", 'Japhet Nimmo'. 'Spec's Diarie', and a flood of Manchester sketchery in the papers. He is now Sub-Editor of the Stockport Mercury. He is a man of very fertile and agile mind, with a great deal of that scarce quality (at least in Manchester) simple purity combined with it. He walked home with me from Pendleton to Hulme, at Ten o'clock in the moonlight. His tongue was as glib as a lamb's tail, and I was not in the mood.

SATURDAY, 20TH APRIL, 1850. – Spent the major part of the day at Scott's, discussing with the Radicals, Rhymers, Stowellites, and Teetotal writers and orators that crowd there, especially on a Saturday. – The all engrossing topic both here and wherever I go, seems to be 'The Education Question', and the whole country is now evidently mustering to make this the great centre of all the disputes of the 'Conservative' parties of all shades, on the one hand, and the 'Liberals' and men of progress, reformers, republicans, chartists, annihilators, dissenters, freethinkers, and that vast number of men of all other names who are sickened with things as they are ['on the other' inserted]. Our Committee are active, prompt and bold ['and our views are spreading like wildfire' inserted]. The Church-party are alarmed, and lashing themselves in action and virulence. – Where will it end? In mighty changes, – and, I confidently believe, in good. Providence has a hand in all these things, and purposes at work in them, of which we do not dream. Happy he whose heart rests securely on the wisdom of love of the universal government, and whose constant effort is to act in accordance with it. – In the evening, I went with a young lecturer, of the name of Gawthorpe to see the new Play 'Retribution'. The scenes are laid in the times of the 'Cavalier' and 'Roundhead' war, and this gives some interest to the piece. – This is but the 2nd time of its appearance on this stage, and the actors are anything but up to the mark in emboding [sic] the spirit of it. – The worst blunder in the acting is in the denou[341]ement, – a solemn finale, in which destiny defeats the plots of the designing villain of the piece (Sir Baldwin), and overwhelms him with dreadful penalties, in midst of which a noble old cavalier (Sir Robert Raby) bursts out into a jolly old song of the times in triumph over his fallen foe, from whose dark machinations he has so narrowly escaped:

> The King's a good King, and the Commons are fools,
> And the right boys shall push all the wrong from their stools,'

With an infinitude of unseemly 'Fol de rol' at the end of it, mingled with most uncavalierly cavierly [sic] capering up and down the stage. This, too, looks the worse from being so ill in keeping with the magnanimous deportment of the old soldier through the whole previous part of the play. – At the end of the play, I felt no disposition to see the after piece 'The Serious Family' so I came off, and down to Scotts. – Old Ridings the Poet gave me some advice on Diet and Regimen for men of the scribe genus which so completely accorded with my own experience, that I determined to act upon it. – Wrote a letter of introduction to David Winstanley, Sir Benjamin Heywood's Agent at Miles Platting, for our poor friend 'Dr Primrose', the Yorkshire Grammarian, asking Winstanley to procure him some teaching there. I was glad to hear that Winstanley laid my letter before the Committee of the Institute there, and interested himself very much on behalf of the worthy old man. – Found my rhyme, and my letter to Stowell, in the Spectator today. – Finished the day in a manner unworthy of myself, and went home repentant, and sad. – O God, help me! – I had a chivalrous romance of Old Spain with me to read, – and Carlyle's ['Latter Day' inserted] Pamphlets. –

[342] **SUNDAY, 21ST APRIL, 1850.** – Spent the day in undisturbed silence at my lodgings. Occasional solitude, – frequent solitude, I have ever naturally inclined to, and I have always found it an atmosphere of wisdom and purity in which my errors have been reproved, my thoughts and inspirations uplifted, and my best resolutions strengthened. – I occupied the greatest part of this with writing notes of the week's transactions, with writing a song, arranging my loose papers, and reading 'Mercedes of Castile' by Cooper. About 8 o'clock, I walked out into the quiet lanes and shades of Greenheys to meditate on my

condition and prospects. The night was calm, and clear; and the moon was bright in the deep blue sky, and straggling, snowy clouds were sailing athwart her light in the east. I felt as if everything was beautiful but me ...

More self-recrimination fills the rest of the Page. Page 343 contains a melancholy poem. Page 344 is a heading for the 'District Tea Party Committee at Mather St' but only two receipts for the meeting follow.

[345] **MONDAY, 22ND APRIL, 1850.** – Took Song ['*Poem*' deleted] to the Spectator. – Dispatched Petition to Ashton for the Public Meeting in the evening, to be addressed by Rev. Wm McKerrow, Peter Rylands Esqr, and R. W. Smiles Esqr. – Went home early in the evening to dress for the party at Chorlton Hall. – Pleasant evening, there till ½ past eleven, when I walked home in the moonlight, thinking miserably of the difficulties of my situation with respect to demands for money I owe to different persons who have waited long and patiently. Sad apprehensions. – I must go seriously to work immediately. – I had occasion to see Mr. Howe of the firm of Saml. Fletcher & Sons, and while walking about the third floor of their immense warehouse, I overlooked the whole back part of the Infirmary. It was just noon, and I saw the female relations of the sick inmates coming out from visiting their husbands, brothers, and other friends. They every one seemed affected, but mostly were weeping. – The scene touched my heart with sympathy for the sorrows of the affectionate, and led me into a train of sad musings ... [*More melancholy reflections fill the rest of the day's entry.*]

[346] **TUESDAY, 23RD APRIL, 1850.** – Languid all day in body, but busy in mind. – I was at Scott's, in the Smoke Room at 10 at night, when Elijah Dixon came in, and we debated the Education Question till 12. – Moonlight!

WEDNESDAY, 24TH APRIL, 1850. – Read Emerson's 'Goethe, or the Writer'. – Went to the theatre in the evening. 'Merry Wives of Windsor' 'Prima Ballerina' in which Bonny Miss Payne figures, and an interesting after piece, called 'An Object of Interest'. – Walk into Salford. – Oyster Cellar in Bridge Street.

THURSDAY, 25TH APRIL, 1850. – Had a great deal of dull writing to do today. – Went to Scott's at noon to get my dinner – Ridings, 'Secretary Jones,' old Levers, the ultra-church tee-total advocate,

Welch Williams, the Stowellite, and 2 or 3 strangers were there. After some desultory skirmishing palaver between Ridings, a rough young agent of the National Temperance Provident Life Assurance, and myself, the conversation settled down to the consideration of the natural characteristics of the Lake Country, interspersed with descriptions of Wordsworth and his cottage, and its environments, and of Wordsworth's companions, – The Lake poets and writers, – Southey, Coleridge, and his son Hartley; Wilson; De Quincey; and Harriet Martineau. Such of us as had seen Wordsworth, and the beautiful land of his heart, which was also the text of his genius, were warm upon the theme. – for me, the visit I once paid to that enchanting country is too deeply written upon my memory ever to effaced [sic] in this life; and when country scenes are talked of, it takes the top of my experience, and fills my mind, as the heavenliest piece of this world that kind providence ever blest my eyes with. Its wonderful beauty never rises in my mind but I feel an increased love [347] of all that is good and beautiful in the soul and rise with it within me. Looking back upon my lifetime, and without feeling any prejudice against the ['great' inserted] forms of religion, which in my mind have ['even' inserted] higher utility than the bald asceticism of some of the most puritanical sects allow, – nor men [?] with any wish to insinuate a slight of those persons ...

The diary continues with a scarcely coherent attack on the abuses found in conventional religious practices ...

I will say that the few days I spent, now ten years since, in the Lake country, has done more towards reclaiming me from evil, and impelling me towards all that is excellent in thought and action than all the sermons I ever listened to in that time, and all the potential reading and wrangling I ever engaged in. The remembrance of the looks that nature wore in that region rise in my thoughts by the fire-side, in the street, in the market, in railway-carriage, debating-room, public meeting, and lonely walk, like an angel to reprove me and cheer me. – Men must not tell me that there is only one Gospel revealed in this wonderful world of ours, and that in the Book, that all else is dead. – They are dead who think so. – On this subject then, we were talking at noon, when the little lad with the green Robin-Hood hat on, which hat is known in these days by the slang name of the

'Wide-Awake', came into the doorway, as usual, at that hour of the day, with an armful of papers, and, throwing one on the nearest chair, he shouted out 'Times!' and bolted. The young agent from London, who was 'hard-up' for excitement, and eager for an earful or a mouthful of anything to break the unhappy monotony of his Manchester existence, and who, as he had told me before, was 'dying with ennui' [348] procured the paper. And after navigating his eyes lazily and safely through an ocean of 'debate' and 'foreign' and up and down little streams of 'commercial' and creeks of 'correspondence' and even having approached the rapids, known by the name of 'wanteds', without finding a port into which he could enter, and cast anchor, suddenly shouted out, 'hollo', 'Death of the Poet Wordsworth'. We all started, astounded, and perused the reader's face. – It was so. Wordsworth, whose name was not yet off our lips, and whose virtues and genius were yet thrilling our hearts with blending reverence and pride, was dead, and gentle mother Nature, whose favourite Poet and Priest he had lived, was kindly taking back the mortal relics of her heaven-inspired child into her arms again. The news came like a knell from the spirit land, and we listened to the long newspaper obituary of the bard, with intense interest. – When it was finished, we spoke of him again, but with saddened feelings, and in a lower tone – Some had a touching quotation from the works to allude to. – All that related to him flashed with double vividity upon the memories of those who were in any way acquainted with him. I turned to Ridings and said, 'Elijah, the Bards are going, your head is white, get ready' – We conversed a few minutes on 'The Immortality of the Soul', and then, each in solemn thought, went on his way.

FRIDAY, 26TH APRIL, 1850. – Unwell all day. – The Milton Society met in the evening. – Resumed debate on 'The Education Question' – Smart sparring till 10 o'clock. – Mr. Smiles came in from Preston half an hour before the close of the discussion. – He gave us a short speech.

SATURDAY, 27TH. APRIL, 1850. – Collecting English, French, and Prussian Statistics for the use of 'Little Mirabeau',³ at the approaching Public Meeting in Halifax. – Read Carlyle's 'Model Prisons,' – a

---

³ John Stores-Smith. See note in People and Places.

solemnly-earnest pamphlet for the consideration of this benevolent generation. – Saw my rhyme in the Spectator. – My heart and soul wants mending.

Page 349 has a heading 'Essay on Self Denial', but is then blank. Page 350 is headed 'Our Thoughts are heard in Heaven'

[351] **SUNDAY, 28TH APRIL, 1850.** –I was up late this morning, and when up, felt ill and miserable. – Went out for a short walk in Greenheys till noon. – lay down again after dinner, and read Cooper's 'Headsman' till I fell asleep. Slept till 3. – Got up, mazy, and mazy all over. – Shaved, and washed, and put as good a face on as I could. – Gawthorpe came to tea at ½ past 4. I was as dull as a half-baked brick. – He read criticques [*sic*] on Carlyle by Dr Lees, of Leeds. – Took a walk together through the fields till Eight o'clock. – Went, then, to Chorlton Hall, where Gawthorpe made a 'spout'. – Felt sick of platform twaddle of all sorts. Sick of nostrums and humbugs of all descriptions. – Devilish sick of <u>myself</u> in the first place … [*More introspection follows …*] Walked down to Scott's. – The night was clear [*'and cold' inserted*], with still, sombre, clusters of clouds over the moon. Everything wore a contemplative look. – Sat at Scott's an hour. – Supt there. – What an uncouth squad these teetotalers [*sic*] are! With so little sense, or sensibility about them.–

MONDAY, 29TH APRIL, 1850. – Spent an hour or two, gilding a secret sorrow with a smiling face. – The Barber's shop.[4] – The omniscient heavens are pointing at me! O, miserable man that I am. –

[352] **TUESDAY, 30TH APRIL, 1850.** – A day of perpetual motion, both in mind and body. – Got home at Ten o'clock, and to bed at Twelve, for a wonder.

WEDNESDAY, 1ST MAY, 1850. – As I lay in bed I heard the bells round the necks of the horses from the country, ringing in May morning. – Got to town at Eleven. – hammered my brains a while for some verses to be written in Miss Lucy's Album. – I was not in the vein. – My life is destroying my soul. – I am getting entangled with [*'lathered with' deleted*] a barber [*two words deleted*] to-night.

---

[4] This seems to be one of several oblique references to sexual encounters during this period.

THURSDAY, 2ND MAY, 1850. – No smoke, no snuff, – writing to day. – Read Columbus's Voyages of Discovery 2 hours at Scott's. – Went home at 11?, and worked at a rhyme an hour. – I have had no snuff, nor smoke today, thank heaven, – Sad thoughts. –

FRIDAY, 3RD MAY, 1850. – No snuff nor tobacco to day. – Letters to Wakefield and Rochdale. – It is now night again, and I have disgraced another day ... [*More self-recrimination follows.*]

SATURDAY, 4TH MAY, 1850. – Avoid smoke, snuff and Scott's today. – At the office till Four. Wrote in Miss Lucy's Book. – Morris, and a large company at Scott's. – Game of Reminiscing amongst us. – A runaway Apprentice's visit to the Sea. – An episode in my own life.[5] – Discussions on the Atomic Theory, on the infinitive Mood, and on Baptism, – with illustrations. – Chatwood and Frost.

SUNDAY, 8TH MAY, 1850. – Went to Scott's to breakfast. – Discussion on Milton and Young with readings. – Music. Walk into Broughton, over that river and back through Peel [355] Park. Afternoon at Scott's. – American Discoveries –

Page 353 contains a deleted poem. Page 354 is blank.

[355] **MONDAY, 6TH MAY 1850.** – No snuff, nor tobacco, nor barbarous customs to-day. – Temperance in deed. – Went to the People's Concert in the Free Trade Hall, in the evening. Strong presentiments arising out of my mode of life, and my whole condition. – a mad shaver – * * * * *

TUESDAY, 7TH MAY, 1850. – No snuff, no smoke, nor [*word deleted*] battle with the barber – x x. Dragged myself about my business with a mind full of gloom. – Racking to death with anxiety and sorrow. – I must by a desperate effort rid myself of these dreadful incubuses or they will drive me into the ground. – Received a letter from ['*Dawson of*' *inserted*] Wakefield, accepting my terms of payment of that debt. – A fireside conversation between two old women at Scott's.

WEDNESDAY, 8TH MAY, 1850. – Stuck close to the desk till 3 – Snatched my dinner at Scott's. – Back again and at it till Six. – Scott's

---

5 Waugh did indeed 'run away to sea' as a boy, but soon turned back. (Milner 1893)

to tea. – Too dull for much talk; besides I feel a growing disgust at the tone of the company that frequent the place. – The ignorant vanity, and coarseness of the Teetotal clique, and the still more palpable vanity, and contemptible spongery of old R – . – I felt oppressed with a multitude of painful, and involved anxieties. – Debts, domestic unhappiness, and devilment of all descriptions, including my outward life and inward condition. – Tried to touch up a rhyme which I wrote several years ago. – Am I wasting my time in miserable efforts at versification? – something within me, whether vanity, or a presentiment founded on good judgement, I know not, – would fain answer 'No, go on.' – Whether I [356] am destined to write anything worth reading, I cannot say, but I continually hope for it, and to muse, and try to write my musings and my feelings, is a delight I cannot forego. – But, I shall never do anything great till my heart and life is mended. – I am a self-indulgent slave. – While I live, I cannot, will not rest till I am a better man in heart and thought than now. – to the utmost of my power, I will pay all debts, of all kinds, that I owe, on earth, and in heaven, before I die! – O God, help me in this struggle; for without thy gracious aid, my own effort will be futile. – Went to hear Dr. Mainzer's 1900 Pupils sing in the Free Trade Hall. – I am always affected for good by music, but this great multitude of pretty young melodists delighted me uncommonly. – Passed the barber's shop with the help of the music, but fell into the Snuff-box.

Thursday and Friday I neglected to make any note of.

SATURDAY, 11TH MAY. – Spent the afternoon in lazy drivel with a parcel of teetotal fools at Scott's. – Went, per ½ past 7 train, to Rochdale. – Saw my mother – glad to find her freer of more pain, and, considering all things, in good spirits. – Wandered about with an unhappy load on my mind. –

SUNDAY, 12TH MAY, 1850. – Went to my sister Ann's. – To Foxholes Lodge. – At night-fall, to Frank Clough's at Briarside – I inquired what I owed the Overseers for the maintenance of my wife up to this [357] date. – He promised to send the account over to me. – Slept at Foxholes Lodge. –

MONDAY, 13TH MAY. – Went to hear Mendellson's [sic] 'Elijah' at the Free Trade Hall. – Pugilistic encounter at the door. – ['Called at' inserted] That damned barber's again. –

TUESDAY, 14ᵀᴴ MAY. – Collecting Subscriptions with all my might all day.

WEDNESDAY, 15ᵀᴴ MAY. – engrossed Petition from the Executive Committee praying the Legislature to send a Commission into Lancashire to enquire into the state of Popular Education there. – The Barber's again. – O hell is laying hold of me. – The Supper in the Welch [*word deleted*]. – Four o'clock. – Sneaking to roost – Ashamed of the day light when I got up, dispirited. – ['*Thursday*' *inserted*] Music at Scott's. – Got the Committees' Signatures to the Petition. – Copying old Minutes of Committee. –

FRIDAY, 16ᵀᴴ MAY, 1850. – Did a little dull copying about four hours, and spent the remainder of the day frivolously at Scott's. – 'Songs and chatter' – Corrected proofs of Elijah Ridings' Poems, now printing at Oathfield and Beresford's. –

WEDNESDAY, 22ᴺᴰ MAY. – Up at 5. – Woke Smiles in the next street. – Early breakfast. – Grey morning. – Off to Ardwick Station. – Start for Wortley park. – Scenery on the way. – fringe of Peak Forest. – Woodhead Tunnel. – Hills and dells. – Wortley. – Wharncliffe Lodge. – Inscription:
'Pray for the soule of Thomas Wortteley Knyght for the Kinggs bode to Edward the Forth Rychard Therd Hen. VII and Hen. VIII houses faults God pardon Wyche Thomas caused a loge to be made hon [358] this crag in the midst of Wharncliffe for his plesor to her the Harts bels in the year of our Lord 1510.' –
The crags, woods, wells, dells, and hills of Wharncliffe. – Fine old well at the Lodge. – The Dragon of Wortley's Den. – The Old Woman's Cot. – Walk back to the village of Wortley, at sunset. – The green shaded cottage with the brook coming through the garden in front of it.
A day or two of miserable hilarity at Scott's chiefly.

FRIDAY, 24ᵀᴴ MAY. – Went from Scott's at One. – Roberts and his 2 daughters. – Oxford Road Station. – The country on the sides of the rail to Bowdon. – Bowdon Church. – View thenceforth. – Stroll through Dunham Park. – Fine Trees. – Chesnut [*sic*] trees in blossom. – Dance. – Earl Stamford's Hall. – Moat. – Greyhound's graves. – Twilight among the woods and fields. –

In this month I engaged with Johnson a publisher to read his proofs. – The 1st I read was a work by Everett, the expelled Wesleyan Minister, – 'The Life of John Daniels.' – I went up to the office and, partly to keep the craft in my hand, I composed and worked off a few copies of anything I had just written, – chiefly in the shape of verse. – I took some pleasure in all this.

THURSDAY. – 6TH JUNE. – Cut down my expences [*sic*] as much as possible. – Got a little garrett [*sic*] in my lodgings made as clean and comfortable as possible. – Made my mind up for a period of hard work, and a solitude most agreeable to my tone of mind, and to my whole wants just now. – Decorated my room a little, – cleaned up the old horse-pistols, and hung them against the wall. – Arranged my books and papers. – Resolved to abandon snuff altogether.

Page 359 has the title and two lines of a poem 'The Blind Man groping for his Wife's Grave'. 360 is blank. The following pages up to 368 are either blank or have just the title of a poem, occasionally with a line or two of the poem to follow. Page 361 has a more complete poem entitled 'Tis hard to forget thee for ever', perhaps referring to Mary Ann.

[369] **FRIDAY, 7TH JUNE, 1850.** – Broke faith with myself, and took snuff, to-day. Weak fool! – I will try again. – Went to our first Educational Meeting at Harpurhey, t-night, with Smiles, my brother Secretary and brother to Dr. Smiles, late editor of the Leeds Times, Geo. Parry, a Swedenborgian Minister, L. Simms, Editor of the Stockport Mercury, and John Thompson, a clever young Leather merchant. – In the Temperance School Room. – A good attendance of working people. – each of us had a short spell at talking. – The people were very attentive, and seemed favorable [*sic*] to the Plan, so far as they comprehended it, which was not far I rather think. – However we said a great deal about it, and left them sufficient explanatory matter in the shape of pamphlets to read, and came away in the cool, balmy, loveliness of a summer's night, chatting merrily by the way. – Went to Scott's to my supper; thence home at 12 p.m.

SATURDAY, 8TH JUNE, 1850. – I will avoid snuff today. –
  '[*Parkes 5/-' deleted*] on a/c
  [*Unreadable deletion*]
  Write to Wakefield

'[*Walk ten miles for exercise*' deleted.]

Started with Thompson at 7 through Greenheys, to Platting, there to Birch, thence to Didsbury, and homeward by Fallowfield at midnight.

SUNDAY, 9TH JUNE, 1850. – Started at ½ past ?, according to agreement, with Thompson, by rail to Bowdon, and, from there, to Rostherne Mere. – The village. – The Vicar of Rostherne. – The Church. – View from the Church-yard. – Stone Coffin. – Wicket Gate. – Rostherne Hall. – White Horse. – The banks of the Mere. – Interior of the Church. – The vicar preparing children for confirmation. – Walk to Bowdon at Sunset. – Bowdon Village. – Evening Service at Bowdon Church. – Altrincham. – Sale Moor. – Stretford. – Brundreth's Beef – Summer midnight walk from Stretford to Manchester.[6]

[370] **MONDAY, 10TH JUNE, 1850.** – Unhappy thoughts about my debts and Mother. – Wrote minutes in the fore part of the day. – Went to the printing office in the evening (Johnson's) and saw Johnson there. – Hardman lugged me into his house to tea, and asked me to read over some proofs of his own work, before going to press. – he enforced silence respecting the authorship. – Graphically written. – It will be well received. – Went with Johnson to the Old Meal House to a Meeting for the reduction of Local Taxation. – The gas went out in the middle of a rabid reformer's speech. – After a second's pause, he rattled on in the dark. – Scott's to supper. – More than ever disgusted with these ignorant, hippocritical [*sic*] teetotalers [*sic*], and dissatisfied with myself and unhappy.

TUESDAY, 11TH JUNE, 1850. – A busy, anxious day. – Collecting Subscriptions. – A good week. – Cobden sends us £5, and a letter of encouragement and advice. He will defend us in the house with all his might, when the real tug comes, and the house is calm enough for it to be done with advantage. – Richard Gardner sends us £10. – He is a shrewd, well-educated man, (in book-education), but too much in love with wit, and gay life, [*'ever*' inserted] to turn the world upside down with anything seriously good. – The Committee in good spirits to-night. – Home at nine o'clock. Polished up my old blunderbuss, and fell to writing a sketch of my trip to Rostherne for publication.

---

[6] This walk became the subject of one of Waugh's earliest published essays.

WEDNESDAY, 12TH JUNE, 1850. – Close at the office today. – [*more self pity follows.*] [371] Went to Scott's coffee room. – My gorge begins to rise at it and the pitiful clique of slaves that frequent it, Higher than I can bear. – I have been thoroughly disgusted with one, – and one of the most plausible-looking of their teetotal <u>advocates</u>, too, – who has just told me, while we were out walking together, that secretly, he did not practice [*sic*] the tee-totalism he professed and advocated; and, after he had told me that, straightway went with me into a country inn, and drunk several glasses of ale. I felt so sickened with the fellow that I cannot bear to see him. I advised him to quit all hypocritical advocacy of temperance, and, for his own sake, if he intended to drink, to do it openly, and give his reasons to his temperance companions for doing so. – at all events, to be the thing he professed, and not a hypocritical skulk. The damned hound saw I did not relish it, and urged me, as he had told me in confidence, not to reveal it. – I promised not to reveal it, but begged him immediately to to [*sic*] act like a man in the matter, and rid himself of of [*sic*] the internal, infernal reflection of such a mode of action. – I cannot bear the sight of him, for though I am no better than my neighbours in some things, still I wish [*'above all things' inserted*] to be so, and I hate the wrong thing either in myself or others, and, I believe condemn it as honestly, and mourn for it more.

THURSDAY, 13TH JUNE, 1850. – The day sped away with me in a fit of unhappy contemplation and regret. – dined at Scott's at Seven in the evening – sicker than ever of the damned monkey-cage. – Out of the frying-pan into the fire; – the sign of the Pole.

FRIDAY, 14TH JUNE, 1850. – Dull, dull and melancholy, with a slow-consuming, and secret grief at the very heart of me. – Hell and the [*deletion*] whiskerando. – I wrestled with a mower. – The mower came down like shot. Writing sketch of my trip to Rostherne Mere.

[372] **SATURDAY, 15TH JUNE, 1850.** – At the office till One. To Hardman's to correct some proofs of his Biographical Sketches, for press. – Took tea with him. – The needle's delay. – Our breeches for the morn. – The dun over the street. – Debts the prince of all devils. – The way to hell. – Dulesgate. – 'I'll gang no mair to your town.' The ['*hellish' inserted*] supper party. – Anguish of mind respecting my wife and child.

MONDAY, 17TH JUNE, 1850. – This, and the following day, close collecting Subscriptions. – My wife and my debts kept my mind in a state of perpetual torture. –

The rest of the entry displays similar distress of mind, and the next entry almost three months later suggests that Waugh's personal difficulties remained acute.

[373] **MONDAY, 2ND SEPT, 1850.** – Received a loan of Ten Pounds from Messrs S.P. Robinson, and William McCall, to-day. – To be repaid in 40 weeks, by weekly instalments of 5/-. – Did a little work at the 2nd number of 'Notable Sights' in Johnson's Printing Office. – Paid Shaw 5/-, Armstrong 3/-, Johnson G Rawson £1, Owen 10/-, Smiles 8/-, Scott 2/? – Bought a Dunieford's Belt 5/-, a walking stick 6d., Spent 2/6 at night among my acquaintances at Scott's. – Merry meeting there. – Cannot forget that blasphemous show-man dodge. The Pulpit Roscius at the Mechanics' Institution last night. – The 14 year-old parson. – A disgusting exhibition.

TUESDAY, 3RD SEP. 1850. – Come what may, no snuff today. – The General Committee met at the Rooms, 3, Cross Street, this evening. Old Henry, the M.P. for South Lancashire, and president of the Association, had just come down from the House of Commons for the recess, and, like most of those who visit that great humbug-warehouse, and especially of those who remain in it long, and try to beat a hopeful little symptom or two out of that vast jingle of foolery, he expressed himself as dispirited and despairing of the Association ever producing the effect upon that body which it aims at. He thought it would not be done in the lifetime of the youngest man present. The old Quaker sat down, but his wet blanket wouldn't fit, and it speedily got the water wrung out of it. There were a lot of the old 'Leaguers' present, who are on our executive committee, – old Dyer, Robinson [*'the blunt and bold' inserted*], who lent me £5 this week, McCall [*'silent resolute and gentlemanly' inserted*], who lent me another £5, at the same time, McCartney, McKerrow, the fiery and eloquent, together with a number of talented and determined new men, – Walker, of Oldham, that courageous church minister, who, sacrificing the sympathy of his class to what he [374] conceived to be the truth of the matter, openly and ably expounded our Plan of <u>Secular</u> Education in his own pulpit, against the attacks of his brother clergy and the Bishop of his own diocese. Long life, and joy to him, both in this world, and for evermore! He is a man! Dr Hodgson, and Dr Watts were there. The first is a clear, polished and logical scholar, but not very fervid, nor bold. The last is an ['active' deleted] acute, self-taught man, who has fought his way through a rough life bravely, but has had everything like fine sympathies and perceptions rubbed off him in the passage. – His is a mathematical mind. He is a great master of the statistics of the Educational Question, and understands the arguments on both sides well, and can deal with them adroitly. Carlyle would classify him among the 'logic-grinders'. His is [sic] pugnacious, and loves opposition, and is happiest when he meets with it. But there is much of what seems to me a coarse hard, grovelling, material philosophy about him. He is a master so far as his head, and his heart, – if he has one, – can penetrate, but his range of true vision is narrow. He is of the earth, earthy. A clever mole, – well acquainted with the 'runs'. Emmott was there too, the active young Quaker from Oldham. He has just returned from the Peace Congress, on the Continent. – We are going into Saddleworth together in a few days, for pleasure. – Tucker was there too, with his long nose, and bland, precise, parsonic whine. But this only a fault of his manner. – There is both pluck and intellectual pith in him. These, and others started to their feet, one after another, after old Henry had finished his whimpering lingo, and expressed their opinion that as the Association had ['started' deleted] set out upon its work upon what it religiously believed [375] to be right principles, it was its duty religiously to pursue its purpose till it achieved it. Their banner had not been raised and their choice little band armed to throw down their weapons, and sink into obscure slavery to the state of they complained of [sic], when the first enemy appeared. Conscious of the rectitude of their object, they were the bold['er' deleted] [sic] to contend for it, and [deletion] sure of triumph, and held it a duty to God, themselves, and the next generation that they should never quit the contest till they had gained their point. – This re-invigorated the sluggish blood of our old President. He jumped – no, he doesn't jump, – he rose from his seat slowly, and by instalments, and doubled his subscription. – He is never behind with his money. – A number of others followed his example, on the spot, and the meeting separated with re-doubled determination to go fearlessly a-head till they given [sic] to the people of England cheap, good, and sufficient Secular education, as well as 'Cheap Bread'.

WEDNESDAY, 4TH SEPTR, 1850. – Wrote a short report of last night's proceedings for the 'Spectator'. – I bought a horse hair belt on Monday last, to scour my skin with in my morning washings, and even by this time, I am ['*very*' *inserted*] sensibly aware of fine influence its use diffuses through my system. My appetite, and my strength are increased, my mind is clearer and activer, and my spirits lighter.

I have read 'Don Quixote' this summer, and chiefly in the quiet, comfortable kitchen at my lodgings, where the morning sun makes bars of gold upon the floor, and where, when the back door is open, we can hear the birds singing, just over the houses, in the groves of Green Heys, hard by. It seems to me, a book [376] so congenial to the summer, that it reads richest then. Many a time have I walked down the town, after rambling in imagination with the gentlemanly old lunatic and his inimitable Sancho on their erratic expeditions, and I have, as I trod the streets of Manchester, had my eyes full of sunny old Spain, with its quaint scenes and swarth sons. It is a book that had made ['*a transient*' *deleted*] summer in many a wintry heart, in many a wintry hour; but, after all, Summer is the time, par <u>excellence</u>, to read Don Quixote. – Spent an hour in Scott's coffee room. – I got £10 ['*additional*' *inserted*] from A. <u>Henry</u> and £5, 5 ['*additional*' *inserted*] from <u>Nicholas Heald</u> today for the Association.

THURSDAY, 6TH SEPTR, 1850. [*actually the 5th.*]– Up at 8. – At Johnson's Printing Office at 9, composing ' Notable Sights'. – At the Association's Office, at 10, preparing full report of Tuesday for Exam. And for the Guardian. – Called to see Jerry Garnett and John Harland respecting the insertion of it [*deletions*] in Saturday's paper. – They both away. – Saw young Houldsworth, with the new crop of hair upon his top-lip. – Another of his damned puppy-freaks! – worked from 6 to 9 on 'Notable Sights'. Walked an hour on Stretford Road. – [*Deletions*]

FRIDAY, 7TH, 1850. [*the 6th*]– Down at Johnson's Office at Eight this morning, working at 'Notable Sights'. – Finished report and sent it to the Guardian, and to the Examiner. – Spent two hours at Scott's at noon. – Wit-battle with Roarke – Smoked too much, and snuffed too much to-day. – Johnson's letter to John Hill. – Painful thoughts continually working in my mind, concerning my wife and child. – Strong desire for more solitary habits, – for a pure [377] and manly life, – for [*'good' inserted*] books and [*'a sweet' inserted*] seclusion, in this Manchester hurly-burly of sin, selfishness, and foolery of all kinds.

'It is the heart that makes the life,'

and I am painfully conscious that my heart has wandered from the simple purity of my childhood, and lost much of the fine emotional capacity which it had in that sweet time.

SATURDAY, 8ᵀᴴ SEPTR 1850. [*the 7ᵗʰ.*] – Went to meet Mr. Baxter when the office closed at Noon. – Dined together at Scott's. – received a note from John Stephens, desiring me to meet him at the Liverpool end of Hunt's Bank Station [*'at 3' inserted*] where his mother would also meet me, and speak with me respecting my letter written to her last week. – Remained at Scott's with Baxter till the time, trying some fine old psalm-tunes. Arranged to start with Baxter by the East Lancashire Railway Train at 5–50 to Rawtenstall, thence by his father-in-law's 'drag' 3 miles through Crawshaw Booth, to Love Clough, further up in the Forest of Rossendale. – Met John Stephens, his mother, and sister, at the station, at ¼ – 3. He was just returning to Liverpool from a fortnight's rest at home, having been ill. – He pressed to visit him [*sic*] in Liverpool, at the end of the next week, which I promised to do. – His sister was going with him. The kind old mother parted with her children, and I with my friends, and the [*sic*] started. – Mrs Stephens desired me to walk with her into the town, which I did gladly, so much is my respect for her intelligent head, and kind, motherly heart. – She questioned respecting my unhappy position with my wife, and I answered her more fully and frankly than I should have been disposed to answer any other person in the world, – except my own mother. – She then gave me a world of friendly advice, in [378] such a wise and kindly strain, that I had much ado, once or twice, to keep the water in my eyes as I went through the streets with her. She parted with me in Dickenson St, whither she was going to see friends of hers; and, in parting, assured me that she would see my wife, and would leave nothing undone in the compass of her power, to serve me in any way. She advised me to read my Bible, and connect myself with some religious congregation. I confest that I was a wanderer, wearing the livery of no creed, nor a familiar face in any congregation, yet frequenting places of religious worship, sometimes, and almost indiscriminately, – with, I hope, no undevout purpose. I revere all forms that are conducive to devotion, but, in my present state of mind, I, often, find my truest devotion arises in solitude. – I parted from the old lady, in my heart, thanking heaven for her. –

Mr. Baxter and I started at 5–50 to Love Clough through Bury, by Chamber House, Sir Robert Peel's birth-place, Grant's Tower, Summerseat, etc, and Rawtenstall, where we left the train, and, somehow, missing the gig which was to wait for us, we had to walk 3 miles, in the fine September twilight, through Crawshaw Booth, up to Love Clough. – We reached his father-in-law's house just at 'th'edge o'dark'.

[379] **MONDAY, 9TH SEPTR, 1850** – Met David Morris at Scott's. – He seems little affected by their late crash. He talked and laughed as usual. But he is not implicated in the affair, as his brother is, who, I understand, has been the financial manager. – Preparing with Subscriptions for tomorrow's meeting. – Worked 2 hours on 'Notable Sights'. Pope's sketch of Alderley is a foolish and unfaithful 'thing of shreds and patches.' –

TUESDAY, 10TH SEPTR, 1850 – Letter from Hepworth, threatening me with law for the £1.9 I have owed him so long. I am most heartily ashamed of owing this money to him so long, – especially under the circumstances, – but, law or no law, my brains are racked every day just now to pay those imperative demands for which I have had law already. I can seldom make a jingle of my own coin in my pocket, half-an-hour together, just now. I will write to him, but that is small comfort to either of us in the matter. – Begin to feel compunction for neglecting to acknowledge Espinasse's letter, with his little paper on Worsley. – Worked 2 hours on 'Notable Sights' – Quarrelled with Johnson's partner for breaking my matter every time I went out and not mending it again. Paid another £1 to Nabbs for John Lee.

WEDNESDAY, 11TH SEPTR, 1850. – Was stunned by Espinasse appearing at the Office door this afternoon, with a knapsack slung on his back. – Took tea together at Wovenden's in Market Street. – Went over to Rochdale with him on Saturday.

SUNDAY, 15TH SEP. – 1850. – Spent the day at Bright's at Rochdale. – Jacob at Ben Rhydding unwell. – Grattan, Law, Espinasse, myself and old Sevier, the famous designer, and mechanician, and inventor of the carpet loom. – We were ['*lounging*' *inserted*] all together ['*coming up*' *inserted and deleted*] on a carpet spread upon the lawn in front [380] of the house/Greenbank) with a jar of Turkish tobacco, long pipes, and meerschaums, etc., Bell's Life, etc., spread about us, and with 'Wide-Awake' hats on when 'Our Representative', John Bright, came through the plantation ['*with his wife*' *inserted*] from the quaker's chapel in the town. – He looked solemn and stately at us, but shook hands with us, and received us with his usual courtesy, altho' he whispered to Espinasse. 'Well now, do you think this very intellectual?' 'Oh,' said Little Diogenes, 'I have been betting on the Leger with Lane all forenoon.' – After dinner, the wine, brandy, etc. circulated freely, and the afternoon was spent even worse than the forenoon. – Sevier was a lascivious old debauchee, and told smutty tales, which Esp. at least, and another listened to with [*deletions*] more disgust than delight. – [*Deletion*] Cards – The puritan servant's horror. – The library. – The plantation. – The harbor [*sic*].

– Ride to Rawtenstall with Baxter. – 3 mile walk to his father-in-law's house at Love-Clough. ['*He is*' *inserted*] One of the Rossendale Printing Company. – The Musicians at the Moorland farm. – Sunday at Love-Clough. – The Chapel on the hill. – The hostler got the 'drag' [381] out and drove us to see 'Pendle Hill.'

Preparations for the Great Conference in October. – Quarrell [*sic*] with Johnson and Gawthorpe. – Ditto with Scott. – Negociations [*sic*] with the Examiner people for the publication of 'Tim Bobbin'. – Peacock, Poulton, and Ireland. – The Editor's sanctum. – Still in debt, about £20. – Mrs. Stephens. – Went to Liverpool to see John Stephens. – Visit to his sister's house in Everton on the Saturday evening. – Hunt for Young. – Slept at Stephen's delightful lodgings at Egremont. – arrival of the Asia. – L's bet. Went to Leasome Castle in Cheshire on the Sunday. – Company of Cantabs at Stephens' to dinner – Music, conversation, endless smoke, Drink, Athletic games on the sands. – Slept at Stephens' again. – A gale at sea in the morn. – Crossed the water at 7, with Stephens. Some ships lost on the coast during the day. – Got to M'chester at ½ past 9 a.m. –

Set Sale to print 'Tim Bobbin' as a pamphlet. – hope it will sell, and relieve me from a debt or two. – five weeks absent from R. – No news. – Sunday at Fuller's – The Association shot up suddenly into ['*symptoms of*' *inserted*] great prosperity in October, just before the Conference.

[382] **FRIDAY, 25TH OCT, 1850.** – Meeting of the Milton Society.
– Johnson's paper on ' Amusements conducive to the Welfare of the
People.' – Calm discussion. – Pleasant night. – To the Office again
at Eleven till ½ past Twelve. Clouds sailing over me. – **OCT 30TH
1850.** [*Wednesday*] The <u>Conference</u> of Gentlemen from all parts of
Britain, who sympathised with our Educational Movement. – Mec.
Inst. Cooper Street. – An uncommon gathering of intelligent, liberal,
and determined men. – Cobden there. – Many influential gentry.
– Dinner at the Albion. – Great rush for Tickets to the Pub Meeting
of the following day. – **31ST OCT.** [*Thursday*] – Pub. Meeting at Corn
Exchange.[7] – Crowded. –A platform full of clever and influential men.
– Hickson Ed. The Westminster Review in the chair. – Dr Bacon, of
America, made an excellent speech. – Cobden spoke. –

Chairman received and read a letter from Mr Lombe of Norfolk,
with a £500 cheque enclosed for the Association. – We got nearly £1000
in the course of the previous fortnight. – 270 copies of 'Tim Bobbin's
Cottage' printed on Saturday, **2ND NOV**, [*Saturday*] and I went over
to Rochdale at night, and sold them to my friends there. – Sent one
to Espinasse, Joe Thinne's private Secretary. – He acknowledged, and
approved it, advising me to [*'send' inserted*] Thomas Carlyle one, with a
letter. [383] I will do so in the morning. – that is, <u>D</u>. <u>V</u>. – to-morrow,
the **6TH OF NOV, 1850** – [*presumably Waugh wrote this entry on
Tuesday 5th. November*]

> 'To-morrow! Methought I heard Horatio
> say To-morrow!

6TH NOVR. 1850. [*Wednesday*]– Wrote to Carlyle, with copy of
'Tim'.
Busy selling 'Tim' to my friends to raise cash to meet urgent demands.
– A nasty business. It sickens me. – Necessity leaves no choice. – to
Rochdale on **SAT. THE 9TH** – Same uncomfortable occupation took
up my whole time. – To Milnrow with 3 doz for Scholefield. – Tea at
Tom Livesey's at 'Well I'th'Lone.' – Slept at Hollands, the Roe Buck
in Rochdale. – My poor old mother gets weak. – It will be a sad time
with me when she leaves this world. – – – . Letter from Cousin Grace in

---

[7] At this conference on the 1st of November, the Lancashire Public Schools
Association was renamed the National Public Schools Association (Axon).

London. – Committee night, **TUESDAY 12TH NOV. 1850.** – Home at night in a contemplative mood. – Smiles's fortune. – The bitterness of my own position. – He is a good-hearted, and a clever fellow. – What is it that brings this galling neglect upon me? – **14TH NOV** – Went to the Wesleyan Education Meeting in Mosley Street ['*canvassing*' *inserted*]. – Sick of the cant-poisoned souls that whined blasphemously there. – Not there, O my unfortunate heart [384] not there! Quid te deficis anima mea? Quare et conturbas mea? **15TH** to Rochdale – Roe Buck inn. – Parsons, Mellor 'My Lord' and myself till 4 a.m. – **16TH** Rose with a headache. – Canvassing in Manchester. – To Rochdale again at night with 'Tim'.

17TH SUNDAY. Met Mallalieu and then old corps at Lowerplace. Tea at Tweedale's. Rummaged an old folio copy of Tindal's <u>His. of Eng</u>. with manuscript notes on the margin by Tim Bobbin. It was his own book when alive. Tried to buy it. Nil. Letter with commission from John Stores Smith, one of the Proprietors of Leigh Hunt's <u>Journal</u> and a friend of mine. The <u>Examiner</u> people paid me £1 for the reprint of my sketch.

List of my Debts:

Watts	3. 14. 0
Balmforth	6. 5. 0
Stell	5. 0. 0
Satterthwaite	1. 14. 0
Dawson	0. 18. 0
Hepworth	1. 0. 0
Loan	2. 0. 0
Stanley	1. 0. 0
Glendinning	0. 12. 0
J&R	3. 5. 0
Owen	1. 14. 0
McKerrow	0. 3. 0
Sale	6. 0. 0

[385] **SATURDAY, 14TH DECR. 1850.** – Dined with John Bolton Rogerson, Elijah Ridings, George Richardson, and Mr. Kershaw at Ralph Hale's in Church Street. To go to Rogerson's to tea at the Harpurhey cemetery next day.

Didn't go. – Was in Rochdale.

MONDAY, 16TH DEC, 1850 – Letter from John Critchley Prince about his new book.

SUNDAY 17TH – To McKerrow's Young Men's Improvement Association with Smiles.

Office – bitterness of heart. – my position of debt – domestic mishap – self denial – body and spiritual weakness – visited Mottram with B – Leigh Hunt's Journal Business – Lecture at Cheetham Hill.

1ST MONDAY IN JAN 1851 [*i.e. 6th of January*] – Scott's explosion. Contemplation on the effects of frequenting his house. – Despicable company. – Thoughts on tee-totalers [*sic*] – Thompson – John Stephens – Rochdale. <u>Boothman</u> – Letter to – Compliments on Tim – Order from Leigh Hunt.

Page 386 is largely taken up with a cutting of the Manchester Enquirer report of the 18th of January meeting of the 'Secular Educationists' meeting at Cheetham Hill which records Waugh's contribution to the proceedings. Then –

JAN. 20TH, MONDAY. – Went by invitation to the Oddfellow's Meeting and Tea Party for the inauguration of their New Free Secular School for the Orphans of their order. [387] Held in the large room in Faulkner Street – McKerrow, Dr Watts, Dr Beard, Robert N. Phillips, Mark Phillips, Right Honorable Thomas Milner Gibson M.P., Alex. Henry, Esq M.P., Councillor Bake, Dr. Ryley Steinthal and a few others on the platform. The new teacher from London, (Shields) is a good fellow. He is doubtless a talented teacher, and 'unaccustomed' as he professes to be, 'to public speaking', he made an excellent speech. The countenance of the above-named gentlemen, and their promises of support, gave the whole affair a first-rate start, and put the praise-worthy strugglers into good heart. I feel great sympathy with their purpose, as I always do with anything that I think calculated to raise the working people to a higher position. I was born and bred among them. I know something of their struggles, and their grievances, and of their thoughts and feelings, and of their follies.

A short poem in standard English foregoing snuff and smoking follows. The next entry is out of sequence.

[388] **18TH JAN** – To Rochdale – Mayor, the Watchmaker and Dr. Watts – Roe Buck to sleep. – My mother! – Her kind advice. – Ann. – My cousin Ellen – The Store – James Smithies. – Tim Bobbin at th'Buck – Old Westall's offer of the Copy-right of his edition for £6. – I recommended Crosskill to buy it. – Said he would on Monday morning. – Met my old master (Mr. Thomas Holden) the little high-Church Man – Salaamed to me like an Oriental. He is a clever financier and business man altogether, but a great slave and fool in religion and politics. He is too far gone now too – he will be so as long as he lives.

21ST JAN 1851 – Executive Committee Meeting – Extraordinary deportment of H. R. Forrest, the arch-mischief-maker and his friends Swanwick and Ginty.

A poem of self-examination continues over onto page 389.

[389] **22ND JAN 1851.** – Annual Meeting at the New Offices. The largest and altogether the best Annual Meeting of the Association yet. Milner Gibson, Cobden, Salis Schwabe, R. N. Philips [*sic*], 'Owd Henry', George Wilson, Robinson, McCall, Dyer, Beard, McKerrow, and a great host of old Leaguers there. A good room. Between three and four hundred seated.

Letter from John Stephens, inviting me to Liverpool on the 1st of February.

Resolved to abstain from snuff and smoking to-morrow.

WEDNESDAY, 5TH FEB. – Since last entry, I have been over to Rochdale, and returned again; as usual, when I visit the town now, sick at heart, except that I always feel purified and cheered after seeing my mother. Visited Bolton to arrange for a Public meeting in the Town Hall there. Took tea with Robert Heywood Esq, the County Magistrate. He shewed me a picture of the Great [390] Pyramid of Egypt, which, he said, it almost made him sweat to look at, even in winter. He had ['*been*' is missing] on a tour in the East, climbed it with the assistance of three Arabs. – His amiable daughter joined us at tea. – Received letters of congratulation for 'Milnrow' from W. M. Young of Liverpool and several other friends (Jacob Bright Jun, Samuel Lucas (John Bright's Brother-in-law,) John Stores Smith, Francis Espinasse, and some others. – It was copied into Eliza Cook's Journal last week, with favourable comments, the Athenaum reviewed it on Saturday last, at length and favourably.

A short indecipherable newspaper cutting follows. The dates which follow are clearly out of sequence.

7TH JAN. 1851. – Meeting of the Milton Society. – Estcourt read an excellent paper on 'The Social condition of the People of Great Britain compared to that of the Continent of Europe, [*deletion*]. Smiles was there.

[391] *Another poem in standard English against smoking and snuff-taking.*

Resolved to smoke not, nor take snuff for a week to come.

SATURDAY, 8TH JAN 1851. – Wrote to Robert Heywood Esq. of Bolton, about the Meeting there. – Wrote special invitations to our friends there, Thomasson of Mill Hill, Ridgway Bridson, John Entwisle [*sic*], and others, as well as to all the dissenting Ministers, asking them to attend the meeting, and requesting the parsons to announce it to their congregations to-morrow. – arrange with a young man from Longsight, of the name of Sharples, to go down to their young Mechanics' Institute there, and give them a lecture on the national Pub School [392] scheme. Listened while Ridings read John Bright's and Lord John Russell's Speeches on the late Papal aggression, and the introduction of a measure into the House to meet the case.

9TH FEBY. 1851 [*Sunday*] – Spent the day in bed till nearly noon, being very much indisposed. – Went to tea to Tom Rowbotham's. James Baxter and his little lad there. Abundance of Sacred Music on the flute and a very fine accordion. – Slept till Ten. – Wrote a letter to Mr. Lucas. – Didn't send it.

10TH FEBY, 1851. [*Monday*] Letter from Butterworth & Co, Law Publishers, London, for a copy of <u>Tim Bobbin</u>. Great Meeting of our Association in the Corn Exchange. Fox spoke at great length, but more tamely than usual. McKerrow opened with his usual pitiful stereotyped vain remarks about 'at this late hour of the night, Mr Chairman', and 'suffering as I am under severe indisposition' and 'I have no intention to make a speech', and then – knowing the laugh it would raise – stripping off his overcoat with energy, – and entering pell-mell into an animated harangue of some length, and ability. Peter Rylands spoke with his usual sense and force and clearness.

The noble church minister, – The Rev Wm. Fullerton Walker, of Oldham, delivered a good speech. The place was filled. Gall! Gall! Gall!

At this point the diary largely becomes a series of blank pages. A cutting from 'The Birthplace of Tim Bobbin' is to be found on one page, and a form for subscribing to Waugh's 'Poems and Songs' dated 1888, and giving Waugh's address as Church Road, New Brighton, with part of a dialect poem written around it is on Page 397. The remaining pages up to 424 are empty, 425, the last page, has a quotation from Emerson and one or two jottings.

A suitable ending to this edition, however, would be the interesting dialect poem which appears on page 395. In form and subject matter it is typical of the poems which later made Waugh famous throughout Lancashire and beyond.

Last Setterdo neet, soon ur th'factory're o'er,
Aw went whom, un wesht mo, un cou'd eawt my hure,
Donn'd my hallady shoon, brusht o'th'flur off my quot,
An lapt up some moufin un cheese in a cleawt,
        An aw sed to hir Mall,
        Neaw then sattle thysal,
For awm beawn't have a bit ov a spree.

Fro week end to week end, fro morning to neet,
Aw bin rivin un tearin for clooas un mheyt,
Fro th'factory to bed, un fro bed back to wark,
My yed's gettin' addle't, my limbs are ur stark
        Ur a poker; bi'th'mon,
        Thea my shap ur ta con,
But aw mun have a bit ov a spree.

Aw [*deletion*] ceow'rt lung anuf wi' my theawm i'my meawth,
Harrish't un parrish't i'th'days o'my yeouth,
['*To get*' *deleted*] For fustian un clogs, un a roof to my yed,
Waytur-porritch un traycle, un strae for a bed
        Bwoth hard wark un hunger,
        Aul ston it no lunger,
Aw mun have a bit ov a spree.

Postscript

Various excerpts of later entries to Waugh's Diary are to be found elsewhere than Manchester Central Library. Principally, in Rochdale Local Studies Library (holding 13468A) there are excerpts from such entries, unpaginated, which Waugh seems to have drawn together just before he died. Two points of interest among these are his visit to the Great Exhibition in 1851, and a meeting with Samuel Bamford, the Peterloo radical, in 1854.

His incomplete description of the Exhibition, which gives familiar descriptions of its wonders, is less interesting than his account of his visit to the house of his hero Carlyle, which he wrote when drawing his papers together:

In the year 1851, I went up to London, to see the great [*sic*] Exhibition, in Hyde Park; and I took with me an introduction, which, if I remember right, was from my old friend, Mr. Alexander Ireland, to Thomas Carlyle, of Cheyne Row, Chelsea. During my stay in London, I resided with an old aunt of mine – my father's sister, Elizabeth, – at the village of Stepney. – Very soon after my arrival I made my way down to Cheyne Row, but, when I got to the house, – such was my professional veneration for the famous sage of Chelsea, that I was almost afraid to knock at the door. – At last, however, I ventured, and the door was opened by a tall clean, staid-looking old Scotch servant, who, to my great relief, told me that Mr. Carlyle was away in the Isle of Wight, and would not be back for a fortnight. – And so I missed the only chance I ever had of seeing the famous man whose writings, especially 'Sartor Resartus', had made a great impression upon me.

His somewhat thorny meeting with old Sam Bamford in 1854 makes another interesting postcript to the earlier diary entries.

25TH OCT 1854

Sam Bamford in Manchester, on a visit from London – He has been twice to our place for me. – He dined with Cooper, the bookseller, one day lately, and asked where I could be seen. I left a card with Cooper saying where I would meet him – at 1, Spring Gardens, any hour from 9 a.m. to 6 p.m. or at the Shandean Club, on Saturday night. – He missed me – Espinasse wants to see him also.

26TH OCT, 1854 – In the evening I went out to Sam Bamford's old haunts to see if I could find him. – Went up to Charles Riding's house, the "Royal Oak" in London Road. Sam was not there, nor at the "Thatched House". I called also upon Espinasse, at his editorial <u>sanctum</u>. Sam had not been there; and having no likely clue to his whereabouts, I gave up the search. Called in Smithy Door to buy some cupboard gear and went down Deansgate in the rain, intending to get on the first 'bus going my way. As I passed the "Three Arrows", I thought I would look in once more. I enquired at the bar, and the landlord (Beilfe?) told me that "Mr. Bamford" was "in the room there." I entered, and there sat old Sam with his hat off among a small company, most of old acquaintances of his. His hair lay in white, disorderly masses about his large head. His rugged, manly old Lancashire face looked thinner than formerly, and began to shew its bony frame-work. He was well-dressed, with a touch of the gentleman about his garb. He used to delight in an air of comfortable rusticity in his attire. His broad manly figure was still upright and striking. My great-coat and old broadbrimmed hat disguised me a little; and, when I went up to him with my hand offered, he stared and said "Who are you?" I doffed my hat and sat down beside him. He instantly recognised me, and giving me a hearty shake, he said aloud, "Eh, Edwin, my lad, is that thee! Aw'm fain to see tho. What, aw've bin lookin for tho, up an deawn th'teawn." He drank up, and called for fresh glasses. I pressed to pay for them on the score of his being a visitor; and put down half-a-crown. "What," said he, "has theaw had a fortune left tho, or summat, at theaw throwes deawn thi medal so fast!" After many united[?] [*'personal' inserted*] enquiries; our conversation glided to other topics, and he began to express his dislike of London, and [*'Londoners, its society' deleted*] and his disgust at the stupid drudgery of his occupation. He told me that he had abundances of matter in his possession, which, if he were in his native place, and at leisure, he could work up into a valuable contribution to the literature of Lancashire before he died. But his sun was getting to the setting; and he believed the wealthy men of the country did not care to have such a service done; and they would rather see a man like him grind out his days in a stupid employment which any blockhead could do just as well as he. His language was clear, and vigorous, and full of striking original metaphor, and it smacked, as it ever did, of his natural dialect. We left the "Three Arrows", and went together to the "Thatched House" to meet Espinasse, as I knew he was likely to call there. He was not there when we went in, and we sat down. – Sam was getting a little elevated and [*deletion*] talked with bitter strength of Espinasse – whom 'he ['*could*' *deleted*] had loved as if he was a lad of his own,' not having written to him, nor sent a single paper to him during all his absence. He asked me about my book[1] ['*and*' *deleted*] what I had got for it, and the like. I happened to have the first sheet of 32 pages in my pocket, which he took with him. He begun [*sic*] to talk to me with me in a tone of patronising, and paternal admonition. He said I was a lad of some talent; and this first book of mine, would either damn me, or set me up as a writer. He advised me to put my powers to a noble use, and if ever I had occasion to write of the ['*manufacturing*' *inserted*] men of Lancashire, or the powers that be, not to spare the truth, nor yet be too prompt [proud?] to blame. While we were talking, Espinasse came walking in, with spectacles on; pale and keen-eyed, as usual. He came up, and with an air of laxness and surprise, he put out his hand to old Sam. Sam hesitated a minute, and looked reproachfully at him – then he took the offered hand. Then Sam ['*with*' *deleted*, '*all*' *inserted*] his characteristic earnestness and ['*vigorous*' *inserted*] peculiarities of speech, upbraided Espinasse with having slighted him by neglecting to communicate with him. He protested all along, how much he loved Espinasse and how little his attachment to him had been ['*appreciated*' *deleted*] recognised in action of late. Espinasse tried to pacify the old bard as well as he could, and whispered to me " This is an extraordinary exhibition of affection. I can't account for this. I used to meet him ['*only*' *inserted*] now and then when in London, – but I never dreamt of anything like

---

[1]   Presumably this book is *Sketches of Lancashire Life* published in 1855.

this." Sam would not be pacified; and, being on the [*'lofty'*, *'excited'* *deleted*] side of sobriety, he still growled out his reproaches, mingled with bursts of general defiance to all fleeting friends and proud men. Espinasse got fidgetty [*sic*], for he could not join in with the irascible and excited, and offended old poet. At last I rose to accompany Sam to the [*10 o' clock interpolated*] bus at the corner of Cross St, which was to take him down to Pendleton. He shook hands with Esp. heartily, and we went outside. When we got there, he saw that Espinasse had not followed us, and looking round he said, 'Well, what's Espinasse going to do. Isn't he comin?' He refused to stir till he came forth; so I went in for him, and we both accompanied the old poet to his 'bus and took leave of him as he was seated inside.

People and Places

Brief notes on some of the people and places mentioned in the diary.

William **Ardrey** 19+/9/48, 12/4/50. Bookseller in Market Street and also, by Waugh's account, a peripatetic dealer.

Samuel **Bamford** (1788–1872) 25/10/54, 26/10/54. The well-known veteran of Peterloo, and prominent local writer. His relationship with Waugh was never an easy one. Waugh found him pretentious and unreasonable in his behaviour, and Bamford was highly critical of Waugh's treatment of Mary Ann.

James **Baxter** 8/9/50, 15/9/50, 9/2/51. A friend of Waugh, Secretary to Mr. Bateman, engineer employed at Manchester Waterworks, Woodhead. He took Waugh to his father-in-law, Mr. Giles Bury's, house at Love Clough near Rawtenstall on several occasions. Giles Bury was a calico printer. (MS F 828.89 W15 MCR).

Dr. **Beard** 27/9/48, 20/1/51, 22/1/51. A Unitarian and Committee member of the L.P.S.A. (Maltby p. 154).

Betty **Bohanna** 12/4/50. Betty Bohanna (d. 1853), owner of a circulating library, was the estranged wife of bookseller Daniel Heywood. (Powell).

Jacob **Bright** (1821–1899) 11/9/48, 15/9/50, 5/2/51. The younger brother of John Bright. One of the original founders of the L.P.S.A. (Maltby p. 68). Later an MP for Manchester and supporter of Women's Rights. (D.N.B)

John **Bright** (1811–1889) 19/8/47? 15/9/50. With Cobden, a leader of the Anti-Corn Law League in Manchester, which succeeded in repealing the Corn Laws in 1845. MP for Durham from 1842 to 1847. M.P. for Manchester from 1847 until 1857. (Swindells 3 p. 37, Maltby p. 156). A prominent Quaker and leading politician throughout his life.

Jos. **Brotherton** (1783–1857) 3/8/49. A member of the Ant-Corn Law League and one of the Vice-Presidents of the L.P.S.A. (Maltby pp. 50, 57, 154). He was the first MP for Salford which he represented till his death (Axon).

Thomas **Carlyle** (1795–1881) 1849(2) undated, 2/10/49, 3/4/50, 3/9/50, 2/11/50, 6/11/50, Postscript. The famous essayist and thinker. Writer of *Past and Present, Sartor Resartus* etc. Partly through Espinasse's connection with Carlyle, along with Burns and Emerson he seems to have been the principal literary influence upon Waugh as a writer.

George **Cartledge** 25/9/48. He was an 'old bookseller and picture dealer at 34, Lower King Street.' (Directory 1855)

Richard **Cobden** (1804–1865) 21/8/49, 27/9/49, 11/6/50, 25/10/50, 22/1/51. Cobden was leader with Bright of the Anti-Corn Law League. Though he played little part in the L.P.S.A. in its early years, he took a key role when it became a National Association after 1850 (Maltby p. 80)

W. Sharman **Crawford** 30/7/47, 11/5/48. He was elected unopposed as MP for Rochdale in 1847.

James **Daly** (1811/12–1849) 7/1/48, 8/10/48, 29/10/48, 18/7/49, 21/7/49, 29/7/49. Close friend of Edwin Waugh's, and, as the diary tells us (30/6/49), Secretary of the fledgling Rochdale Cooperative Society and the person who drew up its constitution. 'James Daly was a native of the County of Longford in Ireland. He was a naturally studious and gifted man. He was remarkably witty; a great lover of books, especially of books on abstruse subjects. – He was for many years in the employ of Mr. Thomas Robinson, Joiner and Builder, of Water Street in Rochdale.' (Waugh's *Unpublished Pieces*, Rochdale Local Studies Library). Waugh makes no record of his death in the diary, though he met him more than once in the year he died, possibly because he did not know about his fate. Daly died and was buried at sea (Co-operative Museum Records, Rochdale).

Dr. Samuel **Davidson** 27/9/48, 25/3/50. Professor of Biblical Literature at the Independent College in Whalley Range. He was a member of the General Committee of the L.P.S.A. (Maltby p. 154)

Elijah **Dixon** (1790–1876) 23/3/50, 5/4/50, 23/4/50. Born in Yorkshire, he found work as a young man in an Ancoats Cotton Mill. He was present at Peterloo, was arrested and sent to London for trial. Later he founded a successful business making matches. He climbed Snaefell at the age of 85. (Swindells 5, pp. 216–220)

J. C. **Dyer** 26/10/48, 3/9/50, 22/1/51. A Vice-President of the L.P.S.A. (Maltby p. 154)

Ralph Waldo **Emerson** (1803–1882) 22/11/47, 29/11/47, 1/12/47; 16/9/48, 28/9/48. The well known American transcendental philosopher and writer whose influence on Waugh is very clear. He arrived in Manchester in October 1847 and 'resided' there 'for some months'. He was on a lecture tour of 'various Mechanics Institutions and other literary associations' organised by his friend Alexander Ireland. He came again in 1873. (Axon). More details of his visit to Manchester can be found in R. L. Rusk *The Life of Ralph Waldo Emerson*, 1949 pp. 333–334.

Francis **Espinasse** (c. 1823–1912) 19+/9/48, 16/7/49, 17/7/49, 24/7/49, 27/7/49, 6/8/49, 10/8/49, ?/7/49(2), 30/6/49(2), 22/8/49, 7 /8or9/49, 10/9/49, 11/9/49, 25/9/49, 2/10/49, 3/10/49, 10/9/50, 11/9/50, 15/9/50, 29/10/50, 5/2/51, 26/10/54. Jokingly referred to as 'Diogenes' (the Greek cynic philosopher) (16/7/49) in the diary. A prominent literary figure in Manchester during the second half of the Nineteenth Century. Author of *Lancashire Worthies* (1874). He wrote an affectionate obituary of Waugh, and was clearly an important figure at the time of the diary, both as a friend, and a link to the literary world. He was a member of the General Committee of the L.P.S.A. (Maltby p. 154)

H. R. **Forrest** 15/9/48, 26/10/48, 21/1/51. A member of the General Committee of the L.P.S.A. whom Waugh clearly found particularly exasperating.

W. J. **Fox** 10/2/51. One of the Vice-Presidents of the L.P.S.A. (Maltby p. 154) MP for Oldham. He introduced an unsuccessful education bill in the Commons in February 1850 (Maltby p. 75). A prominent Unitarian and supporter of the Anti-Corn Law League (Uglow pp. 170–71).

Richard **Gardner** (1814–1856) 2/5/48, 26/10/48 5/4/50, 11/6/50. A Vice-President of the L.P.S.A. (Maltby p. 154). Born in Manchester, he was MP for Leicester from 1847 until his death. (Axon)

Elizabeth **Gaskell** (1810–1865) 18/3/50. The novelist had published *Mary Barton*, her first successful and controversial novel concerning Manchester life in 1848.

John **Harland** (1806–68) 6/9/50. Chief reporter and then Editor of the *Manchester Guardian*. He was a noted antiquary and later promoted Waugh's poetry in his anthology *Lancashire Lyrics* (1866).

Alexander Henry 25/3/50, 3/9/50, 4/9/50, 20/1/51, 22/1/51. He was President of the L.P.S.A. and Liberal MP for South Lancashire 1847–1852. (Maltby p. 154, Swindells 2 p. 17)

Robert **Heywood** 5/2/51, 8/1/51. One of the Vice-Presidents of the L.P.S.A. (Maltby p. 154). A County Magistrate in Bolton.

Thomas **Holden** 20/8/47, 26/11/47, 18/1/51. A Bookseller and printer in Rochdale. He was Waugh's first employer.

Charles **Howarth** (1814–68) 19/11/47, 22/11/47, 23/11/47, 2/12/47, 8/12/47, 29/10/48. One of the founders of the Rochdale Cooperative Society. He was its first President and remained politically active throughout his life. (c.f. Internet Co-op on line)

Alexander **Ireland** (1810–1894) 22/11/47, Postscript. Born in Edinburgh, from 1846 he was Publisher and Business Manager of the *Manchester Examiner*, founded in 1845. Ireland instigated and arranged Emerson's lecture tour of Britain in 1847–48 and was the father of the composer John Ireland. (D.N.B.)

Joseph Johnson 4/10/49, 24/5/50, 10/5/50, 2/9/50, 6/9/50, 7/9/50, 15/9/50, 29/10/50. Publisher at 10 Newalls Buildings, Market Street who published much of Waugh's early work as he struggled to make his way as a writer.

Alderman James **Kershaw** 26/10/48, 25/3/50, 14/12/50. A millowner. Elected Mayor of Manchester in 1842. Liberal MP for Stockport 1847. (Swindells 2 pp. 20–22)

Thomas **Lamb** of Wakefield 25/11/47, 7/1/48, 23/9/48. 'The Revd. Thomas Lamb was a Baptist Minister in Wakefield during the time when I was engaged upon the Wakefield Journal. He had a number of pupils who met at his house, for instruction in English Literature and Composition.' (Waugh's *Unpublished Pieces*, Rochdale Local History Library).

James Henry **Leigh Hunt** (1784–1859) 17/12/50, 6/1/51. The well known essayist, poet and editor.

Samuel **Lucas** (1805–1865 or 1870), 1/12/47, 4/5/48, 9/5/48, 11/5/48, 15/9/48, 26/10/48, 5/2/51, 9/2/51. Brother-in-law to John Bright and a fellow Quaker. He was Chairman of the L.P.S.A. According to Maltby (p. 75) his move to London in 1849 was a severe loss to the movement. In 1856 he became editor of the *Morning Star* (Maltby p. 68)

MacDougall the Arithmetician 18/9/48. Presumably Duncan MacDougall, writing master and accountant, 22 Brasenose Street. His wife ran a 'Ladies School' at the same address. (Directories 1848)

Horace **Mann** (1796–1859) 26/11/47, 3/12/47. A prominent American Unitarian educationalist, writer and first President of Antioch College. It is evident that the American influence of Emerson and writers such as Mann was very influential in the thinking of the Lancashire Public Schools Association.

Dr. Joseph **Mainzer** 27/9/48, 8/5/50. 'Professor of Music' in Newall's Buildings, Market Street (Directories 1850)

William **Mallalieu** (c. 1796–1863) 8/10/48, 23/10/48, 24/10/48, 29/10/48, 5/11/48, 17/11/50. Owner of a Woollen Mill at Sudden. He was one of founders of the Rochdale Cooperative Society.

Mayor of Manchester 26/10/48, 19/3/50. See Sir John **Potter** below.

Rev. William **McKerrow** (1803–1878) 6/7/49, 25/3/50, 22/4/50, 3/9/50, 17/11/50, 16/12/50, 20/1/51, 22/1/51, 10/2/51. A member of the General Committee of the L.P.S.A. (Maltby p. 154). He was Minister at Lloyd Street Presbyterian Church from 1827 onwards. He worked in Manchester throughout his life, and served as moderator of the Presbyterian Church of England. The initial meeting to found the L.P.S.A. took place at Lloyd Street Church, which stood on the corner of Mount Street, and was sold in 1858 (Maltby p. 68, Swindells 1 pp. 255–256) An original proprietor of the *Manchester Examiner*.

T. **Milner-Gibson** 12/4/50, 20/1/51, 22/1/51. He was M.P. for Manchester from 1841 to 1857 (Maltby p. 156)

Rev. Richard **Morris** 26/10/48, 6/7/49. He was minister at York Street Baptist Chapel. (Directories 1848).

Mark **Phillips** 20/1/51. MP for Manchester 1832–1847. A prominent Wesleyan and a supporter of the L.P.S.A., although many Wesleyans were opponents (Maltby pp. 49, 56)

Sir John **Potter** 26/10/48, 19/3/50, 4/4/50. Mayor of Manchester between 1848 and 1851. With Dr. John Watts he was inaugurator of the Free Library system in Manchester in 1852. He was knighted on Queen Victoria's visit to Manchester in 1851. He became MP for Manchester in 1858 but died shortly afterwards. (Swindells 1 p. 251, 3 p. 159)

John Critchley **Prince** (1808–1886) 16/12/50. Born in Wigan, he was a local poet, writing in standard English, of considerable reputation. (Maidment p. 338)

Elijah **Ridings** (1802–72) 11/8/49, 10/3/50, 6/4/50, 20/4/50, 25/4/50, 15/5/50, 14/12/50, 8/1/51. A well-known local poet and bookseller. Referred to by Waugh as 'old Ridings the poet' (20/4/50), and warned on the death of Wordsworth 'Elijah, the Bards are going, your head is white, get ready,' (25/4/50) but actually then only 48 years old at the most.

Smith Phillips **Robinson** 2/10/49, 2/9/50, 3/9/50, 22/1/51. A member of the General Committee of the L.P.S.A. (Maltby p. 154).

John Bolton **Rogerson** (1809–1859) 14/12/50. A local literary figure and Registrar and Chaplain at this time of Harpurhey Cemetery (Directories 1850). He was author of *Flowers for all Seasons* (1854).

Lord John **Russell** (1792–1878) 3/4/50, 4/4/50. British Prime Minister from 1846 until 1852.

Salis **Schwabe** (1800–1854) 22/1/51. Owner of a Calico Printers. He was a member of the General Committee of the L.P.S.A (Maltby p. 154). A Unitarian and a close friend of Mrs. Gaskell (Uglow p. 161).

R. W. **Smiles** 22/4/50, 26/4/50, 7/5/50, 22/5/50, 12/11/50. 'My brother secretary and brother to Dr. Smiles late editor of the Leeds Times' (7/5/50) i.e. brother of the author of *Self Help* (1859), *Lives of the Engineers* (1861) etc … He was involved in Secretarial duties with the Association until its dissolution in 1862, and was given £60 of the £260 which still remained in the funds (Maltby p. 94). He was librarian of the Manchester Free Library from 1858 to 1862 (Axon).

Rev. William Saltmarshe **Smith** 17/08/47, 4/10/47, 9/5/48, 7/9/48, 8/9/48, 19+/9/48. Minister at Blackwater Street Unitarian Chapel in Rochdale from 1843 to 1859. (*Rochdale Unitarian Manual*, 1893 p. 30) He was Waugh's Latin teacher, and later sent threatening letters and brought court proceedings for non-payment of lesson fees.

James **Smithies** (1819–1869) 18/1/51. A prominent and active founder member of the Rochdale Co-operative Society.

Thomas **Sowler** 10/9/47. Editor of *The Courier* 4 St. Ann's Square. The *Courier* was printed every Saturday. (Axon 1886)

Dr. Ryley **Steinthal** 10/3/50, 20/1/51. A member of the General Committee of the L.P.S.A. (Maltby p. 154)

John **Stores-Smith** 10/9/49, 25/3/50, 17/11/50, 5/2/51 (Maltby pp. 75, 107). The author of 'Mirabeau and Social Aspects', from whence his nickname. A member with Waugh and Espinasse of the Shandean Club in the early 1850's. (Powell).

Rev. Hugh **Stowell** (1799/1800–1865) 27/3/50, 12/4/50, 20/4/50. Born in the Isle of Man, he came to Lancashire in 1828 as Curate at St. Stephens Salford. He then became Vicar of Christ Church, Salford, a church built by his supporters, in 1831. A prominent Anglican Churchman with robust opinions. (D.N.B.) He vehemently opposed the Plan, and led the powerful opposition to it.

Charles **Swain** (1801–1874) 15/9/47, 27/3/50, 12/4/50, 20/4/50. A well known Manchester born poet, who had made a literary career in London. (Maidment p. 121).

Dr. **Vaughan** 27/9/48 The Reverend Robert Vaughan, Professor of Theology at Lancashire Independent College.(Directories 1848)

Henry **Vincent** (1813–1878) 18/4/48, 2/5/48. A prominent Chartist, who stood as a Radical for Parliament in several constituencies during the 1840s and was a well known and powerful itinerant speaker. (Internet: National Archives)

Dr. John **Watts** (1818–1887) 1/12/47, 26/10/48, 1/10/49, 3/10/49, 25/3/50, 12(15)/4/50, 3/9/50, 17/11/50, 18/1/51, 20/1/51. He was one of the 12 sons of a Coventry ribbon-weaver. He came to Manchester in 1840 as a paid lecturer in the Owenite cause and was a 'professed agnostic' (Maltby p. 75). Maltby describes him as 'the moving spirit of the Executive Committee'. In February 1851 he was appointed full-time agent of the National Public Schools Association and remained active in Educational Reform up to the time of the Education Act in 1870 (D.N.B.). He is also credited with inaugurating the Free Library system in Manchester in 1852. (Swindells 1 p. 251)

James (Jem) **Weatherley** (1794–1860) 29/4/48, 14/9/48, 16/9/48, 19+/9/48, 23/9/48, 4?/10/48, 30/6/49(2), 31/8/49. (Sometimes spelt Wheatherley, or Whetherley by Waugh). Bookseller in Shudehill. Of humble origins, yet prospered for a time as a bookseller, though he died in penury. (Swindells 2).

He also wrote a diary, kept in Chetham's Library which gives an eye-witness account of Peterloo

Roger **Weatherley**, 23/9/48, Jem's son later became an artist and photographer in Sheffield. (Powell) (*City Notes and Queries* 22/3/1879).

Members of Edwin Waugh's family

Mary Ann Waugh. Edwin Waugh's wife. Born Mary Ann Hill 1822 in Littleborough. married Edwin Waugh at St. Chads Church, Rochdale on the 11th of May 1847 (John B. Taylor, genealogist). She was still living in Lower Shore at the time of the 1881 census.

Aunt Sally 1/9/47?, 3/10/48, 5/11/48, 22/7/49, 1/7/49(2), 24/3/50. Mary Ann's Aunt Sarah **Wood**. (see letter MS928 28 W89: Manchester Central Reference Library). Lodgekeeper at Foxholes, the home of the Entwistles in Rochdale and a valuable go-between for the warring couple.

Waugh's mother (nee Elizabeth Howarth) Daughter of William Howarth, stonemason and engraver. As the diary indicates Waugh was the child of her second marriage. She had previously been married to James Hawkward and lived at Midge Hole, Caldermoor (see entry for 22/7/49).

Ann 8/10/48, 21/7/49, 22/7/49, 24/3/50, 12/5/50, 18/1/51 Waugh's half-sister.

Cousin Ellen 18/1/51.

Aunt Ann 22/7/49. A worker with her family at Scholefields Mill. Buckley.

Cousin Grace 9/11/50

Cousin Jack 30/6/49(2)

Uncle Bob 21/7/49, 1/7/49 (2), 19/7/49, 30/6/49(2). His mother's brother, a musician and prominent Methodist. A handloom weaver.

John **Clegg** 3/10/48, 5/11/48, 6/8/49. Mary Ann's Uncle and a grocer in Milnrow.

Sally **Clegg**, his wife 3/10/48, 6/8/49

Places

The Dog and Partridge Inn 22? /7/49, 29/7/49, 30/7/49 The Dog and Partridge Inn at Caldermoor where Waugh met Mary Ann still exists but is now called the **Caldermoor.**

Foxholes 17/1/48, 9/10/48, 8/10/48, 28/10/48, 22/7/49, 6/8/49, 11/8/49, 1/7/49(2), 30/6/49(2), 13/8/49(2), 24/3/50, 12/5/50. The house was situated in Rochdale just off the road to Whitworth. Aunt Sally was a lodgekeeper there. The hall was built 1792 and demolished in 1970 (c.f. *Rochdale Observer* 23/5/70). It was the home of the Entwistles. Their collection of art is mentioned by Waugh (25/8/47).

Independent College 30/4/48. The Independent College was situated in Whalley Range and was completed in 1843. It still stands today as part of the Whalley Range Conservation area.

Jacky Lane Brow Woollen Mill 8/10/48. This is almost certainly Union Mill in Sudden. Sudden Brook is still known locally as Jacky Brook. (Rochdale Local Studies Library)

King William Inn 29/7/49 and in the following week. This still functions as an inn at Shore. It has a date stone on it of 1792.

Knott Mill Fair 6/4/50. A traditional fair in Manchester established at the opening of the Bridgewater Canal in 1761 and abolished as a source of trouble in 1876 (Swindells 1 p. 136) Towards the end of his life, after the fair had been abolished, Waugh wrote a poem *'Going to the Fair'* with this event as its subject. (Hollingworth pp. 36–37).

Manchester Infirmary 22/4/50. The infirmary at this date was situated in Piccadilly.

Scott's 6/7/49, 16/7/49, 19/7/49 5/7/49 (2), 30/6/49, 13/8/49(2), 13/3/50, 14/3/50, 19/3/50, 6/4/50, 20/4/50, 23/4/50, 25/4/50, 28/4/50, 2/5/50, 4/5/50, 5/5/50, 8/5/50, 11/5/50, 15/5/50, 16/5/50, 22/5/50, 24/5/50, 7/6/50, 12/6/50, 13/6/50, 4/9/50, 7/9/50, 8/9/50, 9/9/50, 6/1/51. Despite Waugh's antipathy to teetotallers this familiar meeting place for Waugh when he was estranged from his wife is almost certainly William Scott's City Temperance Hotel at Smithy Door. Scott himself is also referred to several times in the diary.

Bibliography

Axon W. E. A., *The Annals of Manchester*, Manchester, 1886 (also available on Internet)

The Dictionary of National Biography

Hollingworth B., *Songs of the People*, Manchester, 1977

Joyce P., *Democratic Subjects*, Cambridge, 1994

Maidment B., *The Poorhouse Fugitives*, Manchester, 1987

Maltby S. E., *Manchester and the Movement for National Elementary Education 1800–1870*, Manchester, 1918

Manchester Directories 1847–1855

Milner G., *Edwin Waugh* (Manchester Literary Club Papers) Manchester, 1893

Robertson W., *Old and New Rochdale and Its People*, Rochdale, 1881

Swindells T., *Manchester Streets and Manchester Men*, Manchester 1906–8

Uglow J., *Elizabeth Gaskell*, London, 1993

Vicinus M., *The Industrial Muse*, London, 1974

Vicinus M., *Edwin Waugh: The Ambiguities of Self-Help*, Littleborough, 1984